Steck-Vaughn

TABE FUNDAMENTALS

Focus on Skills

LEVEL M Language and Spelling

Reviewers

Victor Gathers
Regional Coordinator of Adult Services
New York City Department of Education
Brooklyn Adult Learning Center
Brooklyn, New York

Brannon Lentz
Assistant Director of Adult Education/Skills
Training
Northwest Shoals Community College
Muscle Shoals, Alabama

Jean Pierre-Pipkin, Ed.D.
Director of Beaumont I.S.D. Adult Education
Cooperative Consortium
Beaumont, Texas

D1557940

Rigby • Saxon • Steck-Vaughn

www.HarcourtAchieve.com
1.800.531.5015

Acknowledgments

Supervising Editor: Julie Higgins

Editor: Sharon Sargent

Associate Director of Design: Joyce Spicer

Supervising Designer: Pamela Heaney

Production Manager: Mychael Ferris

Production Coordinator: Heather Jernt

Senior Media Researcher: Alyx Kellington

Design and Composition: The Format Group, LLC

Photo Credits: P. iv ©Bluestone Productions/SuperStock Royalty Free; p. 2 ©HIRB/Index Stock Imagery; p. 4 ©Bob Daemmrich/The Image Works; p. 6 ©Spencer Grant/PhotoEdit; p. 29 ©Hulton-Deutsch Collection/CORBIS.

Illustrations: Pp. 13, 21 Jim Haynes; pp. 48, 52 Andrew Lankes; pp. 25, 31, 43, 45, 65 Francine Mastrangelo; pp. 9, 50 Bob Novak.

Contents

To the Learner

Congratulations on your decision to study for the TABE! You are taking an important step in your educational career. This book will help you do your best on the TABE. You'll also find hints and strategies that will help you prepare for test day. Practice these skills—your success lies in your hands.

What Is the TABE?

TABE stands for the Tests of Adult Basic Education. These paper-and-pencil tests, published by McGraw-Hill, measure your progress on basic skills. There are five tests in all: Reading, Mathematics Computation, Applied Mathematics, Language, and Spelling.

TABE Levels M, D, and A

Test	Number of Items	Suggested Working Time (in minutes)
1 Reading	50	50
2 Mathematics Computation	25	15
3 Applied Mathematics	50	50
4 Language	55	39
5 Spelling	20	10

Test 1 Reading

This test measures basic reading skills. The main concepts covered by this test are word meaning, critical thinking, and understanding basic information.

Many things on this test will look familiar to you. They include documents and forms necessary to your everyday life, such as directions, bank statements, maps, and consumer labels. The test also includes items that measure your ability to find and use information from a dictionary, table of contents, or library computer display. The TABE also tests a learner's understanding of fiction and nonfiction passages.

Test 2 Mathematics Computation

Test 2 covers adding, subtracting, multiplying, and dividing. On the test you must use these skills with whole numbers, fractions, decimals, integers, and percents.

The skills covered in the Mathematics Computation test are the same skills you use daily to balance your checkbook, double a recipe, or fix your car.

Test 3 Applied Mathematics

The Applied Mathematics test links mathematical ideas to real-world situations. Many things you do every day require basic math. Making budgets, cooking, and doing your taxes all take math. The test covers pre-algebra, algebra, and geometry, too. Adults need to use all these skills.

Some questions will relate to one theme. Auto repairs could be the subject, for example. The question could focus on the repair schedule. For example, you know when you last had your car repaired. You also know how often you have to get it repaired. You might have to predict the next maintenance date.

Many of the items will not require you to use a specific strategy or formula to get the correct answer. Instead this test challenges you to use your own problem-solving strategies to answer the question.

Test 4 Language

The Language test asks you to analyze different types of writing. Examples are business letters, resumes, job reports, and essays. For each task, you have to show you understand good writing skills.

The questions fit adult interests and concerns. Some questions ask you to think about what is wrong in the written material. In other cases, you will correct sentences and paragraphs.

Test 5 Spelling

In everyday life, you need to spell correctly, especially in the workplace. The spelling words on this test are words that many people misspell and words that are commonly used in adult writing.

Test-Taking Tips

1. Read the directions very carefully. Make sure you read through them word for word. If you are not sure what the question says, ask the person giving the test to explain it to you.

2. Read each question carefully. Make sure you know what it means and what you have to do.

3. Read all of the answers carefully, even if you think you know the answer.

4. Make sure that the reading supports your answer. Don't answer without checking the reading. Don't rely only on outside knowledge.

5. Answer all of the questions. If you can't find the right answer, rule out the answers that you know are wrong. Then try to figure out the right answer. If you still don't know, make your best guess.

6. If you can't figure out the answer, put a light mark by the question and come back to it later. Erase your marks before you finish.

7. Don't change an answer unless you are sure your first answer is wrong. Usually your first idea is the correct answer.

8. If you get nervous, stop for a while. Take a few breaths and relax. Then start working again.

How to Use *TABE Fundamentals*

Step-by-Step Instruction In Levels M and D, each lesson starts with step-by-step instruction on a skill. The instruction contains examples and then a test example with feedback. This instruction is followed by practice questions. Work all of the questions in the lesson's practice and then check your work in the Answers and Explanations in the back of the book.

The Level A books contain practice for each skill covered on the TABE. Work all of the practice questions and then check your work in the Answers and Explanations in the back of the book.

Reviews The lessons in Levels M and D are grouped by a TABE Objective. At the end of each TABE Objective, there is a Review. Use these Reviews to find out if you need to review any of the lessons before continuing.

Performance Assessment At the end of every book, there is a special section called the Performance Assessment. This section is similar to the TABE test. It has the same number and type of questions. This assessment will give you an idea of what the real test is like.

Answer Sheet At the back of the book is a practice bubble-in answer sheet. Practice bubbling in your answers. Fill in the answer sheet carefully. For each answer, mark only one numbered space on the answer sheet. Mark the space beside the number that corresponds to the question. Mark only one answer per question. On the real TABE, if you have more than one answer per question, they will be scored as incorrect. Be sure to erase any stray marks.

Strategies and Hints Pay careful attention to the TABE Strategies and Hints throughout this book. Strategies are test-taking tips that help you do better on the test. Hints give you extra information about a skill.

Setting Goals

On the following page is a form to help you set your goals. Setting goals will help you get more from your work in this book.

Section 1. Why do you want to do well on the TABE? Take some time now to set your short-term and long-term goals on page 3.

Section 2. Making a schedule is one way to set priorities. Deadlines will help you stay focused on the steps you need to take to reach your goals.

Section 3. Your goals may change over time. This is natural. After a month, for example, check the progress you've made. Do you need to add new goals or make any changes to the ones you have? Checking your progress on a regular basis helps you reach your goals.

For more information on setting goals, see Steck-Vaughn's *Start Smart Goal Setting Strategies*.

1. Set Your Goals

What is your long-term goal for using this book?

_____

_____

_____

Complete these areas to identify the smaller steps to take to reach your long-term goal.

Content area	What I Know	What I Want to Learn
Reading	_____	_____
Language	_____	_____
Spelling	_____	_____
Math	_____	_____
Other	_____	_____

2. Make a Schedule

Set some deadlines for yourself.

For a 20-week planning calendar, see Steck-Vaughn's *Start Smart Planner.*

Goals	Begin Date	End Date
_____	_____	_____
_____	_____	_____
_____	_____	_____
_____	_____	_____
_____	_____	_____

3. Celebrate Your Success

Note the progress you've made. If you made changes in your goals, record them here.

_____

_____

_____

_____

To the Instructor

About TABE

The Tests of Adult Basic Education are designed to meet the needs of adult learners in ABE programs. Written and designed to be relevant to adult learners' lives and interests, this material focuses on the life, job, academic, and problem-solving skills that the typical adult needs.

Because of the increasing importance of thinking skills in any curriculum, *TABE Fundamentals* focuses on critical thinking throughout each TABE Objective.

The TABE identifies the following thinking processes as essential to learning and achieving goals in daily life:

+ Gather Information
+ Organize Information
+ Analyze Information
+ Generate Ideas
+ Synthesize Elements
+ Evaluate Outcomes

Test 1 Reading

The TABE measures an adult's ability to understand home, workplace, and academic texts. The ability to construct meaning from prose and visual information is also covered through reading and analyzing diagrams, maps, charts, forms, and consumer materials.

Test 2 Mathematics Computation

This test covers whole numbers, decimals, fractions, integers, percents, and algebraic expressions. Skills are carefully targeted to the appropriate level of difficulty.

Test 3 Applied Mathematics

This test emphasizes problem-solving and critical-thinking skills, with a focus on the life-skill applications of mathematics. Estimation and pattern-recognition skills also are important on this test.

Test 4 Language

The Language test focuses on writing and effective communication. Students examine writing samples that need revision, with complete-sentence and paragraph contexts for the various items. The test emphasizes editing, proofreading, and other key skills. The context of the questions are real-life settings appropriate to adults.

Test 5 Spelling

This test focuses on the words learners most typically misspell. In this way, the test identifies the spelling skills learners most need in order to communicate effectively. Items typically present high-frequency words in short sentences.

Uses of the TABE

There are three basic uses of the TABE:

Instructional

From an instructional point of view, the TABE allows instructors to assess students' entry levels as they begin an adult program. The TABE also allows instructors to diagnose learners' strengths and weaknesses in order to determine appropriate areas to focus instruction. Finally the TABE allows instructors and institutions to monitor learners' progress.

Administrative

The TABE allows institutions to assess classes in general and measure the effectiveness of instruction and whether learners are making progress.

Governmental

The TABE provides a means of assessing a school's or program's effectiveness.

The National Reporting System (NRS) and the TABE

Adult education and literacy programs are federally funded and thus accountable to the federal government. The National Reporting System monitors adult education. Developed with the help of adult educators, the NRS sets the reporting requirements for adult education programs around the country. The information collected by the NRS is used to assess the effectiveness of adult education programs and make necessary improvements.

A key measure defined by the NRS is educational gain, which is an assessment of the improvement in learners' reading, writing, speaking, listening, and other skills during their instruction. Programs assess educational gain at every stage of instruction.

NRS Functioning Levels	Grade Levels	TABE (7–8) scaled scores
Beginning ABE Literacy	0–1.9	Reading . . . . 367 and below Total Math . . . . 313 and below Language . . . . . 391 and below
Beginning Basic Education	2–3.9	Reading . . . . 368–460 Total Math . . . . 393–490 Language 393–490
Low Intermediate Basic Education	4–5.9	Reading . . . . 461–517 Total Math . . . . 442–505 Language 491–523
High Intermediate Basic Education	6–8.9	Reading . . . . 518–566 Total Math . . . . 506–565 Language 524–559
Low Adult Secondary Education	9–10.9	Reading . . . . 567–595 Total Math . . . . 566–594 Language 560–585

According to the NRS guidelines, states select the method of assessment appropriate for their needs. States can assess educational gain either through standardized tests or through performance-based assessment. Among the standardized tests typically used under NRS guidelines is the TABE, which meets the NRS standards both for administrative procedures and for scoring.

The three main methods used by the NRS to collect data are the following:

1. **Direct program reporting,** from the moment of student enrollment
2. **Local follow-up surveys,** involving learners' employment or academic goals
3. **Data matching,** or sharing data among agencies serving the same clients so that outcomes unique to each program can be identified.

Two of the major goals of the NRS are academic achievement and workplace readiness. Educational gain is a means to reaching these goals. As learners progress through the adult education curriculum, the progress they make should help them either obtain or keep employment or obtain a diploma, whether at the secondary school level or higher. The TABE is flexible enough to meet both the academic and workplace goals set forth by the NRS.

Using *TABE Fundamentals*

Adult Basic Education Placement

From the outset, the TABE allows effective placement of learners. You can use the *TABE Fundamentals* series to support instruction of those skills where help is needed.

High School Equivalency

Placement often involves predicting learners' success on the GED, the high school equivalency exam. Each level of *TABE Fundamentals* covers Reading, Language, Spelling, Applied and Computational Math to allow learners to focus their attention where it is needed.

Assessing Progress

Each TABE skill is covered in a lesson. These lessons are grouped by TABE Objective. At the end of each TABE Objective, there is a Review. Use these Reviews to find out if the learners need to review any of the skills before continuing.

At the end of the book, there is a special section called the Performance Assessment. This section is similar to the TABE test. It has the same number and type of questions. You can use the Performance Assessment as a timed pretest or posttest with your learners, or as a more general review for the actual TABE.

Steck-Vaughn's *TABE Fundamentals* Program at a Glance

The charts on the following page provide a quick overview of the elements of Steck-Vaughn's *TABE Fundamentals* series. Use this chart to match the TABE objectives with the skill areas for each level. This chart will come in handy whenever you need to find which objectives fit the specific skill areas you need to cover.

Steck-Vaughn's *TABE Fundamentals* Program at a Glance

TABE OBJECTIVE

	Level M		Level D		Level A
	Reading	Language and Spelling	Reading	Language and Spelling	Reading, Language, and Spelling
Reading					
Interpret Graphic Information	✦		✦		✦
Words in Context	✦		✦		✦
Recall Information	✦		✦		✦
Construct Meaning	✦		✦		✦
Evaluate/Extend Meaning	✦		✦		✦
Language					
Usage		✦		✦	✦
Sentence Formation		✦		✦	✦
Paragraph Development		✦		✦	✦
Punctuation and Capitalization		✦		✦	✦
Writing Convention		✦		✦	✦
Spelling					
Vowel		✦		✦	✦
Consonant		✦		✦	✦
Structural Unit		✦		✦	✦

	Level M		Level D		Level A
	Math Computation	Applied Math	Math Computation	Applied Math	Computational and Applied Math
Mathematics Computation					
Addition of Whole Numbers	✦				
Subtraction of Whole Numbers	✦				
Multiplication of Whole Numbers	✦		✦		
Division of Whole Numbers	✦		✦		
Decimals	✦		✦		✦
Fractions	✦		✦		✦
Integers			✦		✦
Percents			✦		✦
Algebraic Operations					✦
Applied Mathematics					
Numeration		✦		✦	
Number Theory		✦		✦	
Data Interpretation		✦		✦	
Pre-Algebra and Algebra		✦		✦	
Measurement		✦		✦	
Geometry		✦		✦	
Computation in Context		✦		✦	
Estimation		✦		✦	

Lesson 1 Objective and Nominative Pronouns

A pronoun is a word that takes the place of a noun. On the TABE you will have to use pronouns correctly. In the correct answer, the pronoun will match the noun whose place it takes.

Example **Look at these sentences. Underline the pronoun in the second sentence.**

Buffalo Bill Cody was an explorer of the American West. He later became a popular showman.

Did you underline *He*? Look at the chart below to see a list of pronouns that can replace the subject in a sentence.

		Singular	Plural
Nominative Pronouns	Take the place of the subject	I you he, she, it	we you they

To replace the noun *Buffalo Bill Cody,* you need a pronoun that is singular, male, and that can be the subject of the sentence. Therefore you use the nominative pronoun *He*.

Example **Look at these sentences. Underline the pronoun in the second sentence.**

Have you heard stories about Buffalo Bill? People tell some wild tales about him.

Did you underline *him*? Look at the chart below.

		Singular	Plural
Objective Pronouns	Take the place of the object of a verb or the object of a preposition	me you her, him, it	us you them

To replace the noun *Buffalo Bill,* you again need a pronoun that is singular and male. This time, however, you need a pronoun that can be the object of a preposition. In the second sentence, *him* is the object of the preposition *about*.

Test Example

Read the sentences and look at the underlined word. Choose the answer that is written correctly for the underlined word.

1   Many people visit Buffalo Bill's grave on Lookout Mountain in Colorado. <u>Them</u> toss coins onto his grave for good luck.

   A It

   B Him

   C They

   D Correct as it is

Hint

Look for prepositions such as *about, above, at, by, in, in front of, inside, into, to,* and *with.*

1 C *They* matches *people*. Both are plural. *People* is the subject of the first sentence, and *they* is the subject of the second sentence. Option A is singular. Option B is an objective pronoun. Option D is incorrect because *Them* cannot be the subject of a sentence.

Practice

Read the passage and look at the underlined words. For numbers 1 through 4, choose the answer that is written correctly for each underlined word.

(1)　　William Cody was born in 1846 in Iowa. By age 11, <u>him</u> was driving wagons across the Great Plains. He became a gold miner, a Pony Express rider, and an Army scout. After he won a buffalo-
(2)　hunting contest, people called <u>her</u> Buffalo Bill.
　　People began to write stories and plays about
(3)　<u>he</u>. You might have read some of them. Not all of the stories were true.
　　In 1882, Buffalo Bill put together a huge show
(4)　about the West. <u>It</u> traveled by train across the United States for more than 20 years. Some say this show was the first rodeo.

1
A he
B she
C they
D Correct as it is

2
F it
G him
H them
J Correct as it is

3
A she
B him
C they
D Correct as it is

4
F You
G They
H He
J Correct as it is

For numbers 5 and 6, choose the word that best completes the sentence.

5 People liked Buffalo Bill's show. Thousands of _____ came to see it.
A it
B him
C they
D them

6 The show also toured Europe. People in England really enjoyed _____.
F it
G he
H him
J them

Check your answers on page 85.

Possessive and Relative Pronouns

A pronoun is a word that takes the place of a noun. Using pronouns helps you avoid repeating the same nouns over and over again. Possessive pronouns show ownership. Relative pronouns refer to a noun or nouns earlier in the sentence. They also connect parts of sentences. On the TABE you will choose possessive and relative pronouns that correctly replace nouns.

Example **Read these sentences. Underline the possessive pronoun in the second sentence.**

Pilar likes to garden. Neighbors say her carrots and radishes are the tastiest around.

Did you underline *her*? Look at the chart below to see a list of pronouns that can show ownership.

		Singular	Plural
Possessive Pronouns	Show ownership	my your his, her, its	our your their

To refer to Pilar, a woman, you need a possessive pronoun that is female. It must also be singular, because she is just one person. Therefore you need the possessive pronoun *her*.

Example **Read the sentence. Underline the relative pronoun that connects the parts of the sentence.**

The man who baked the prize-winning pie was very proud.

Did you underline *who*? Look at the chart below to see a list of relative pronouns.

Relative Pronouns	Refer to nouns; connect parts of sentences	who, whom, that, which, whose, what

Who is the relative pronoun, and it refers to *man*. It also connects the first part of the sentence, *The man,* to the rest of the sentence, *who baked the prize-winning pie was very proud.*

Test Example

Read the paragraph. Look at the underlined word. Choose the answer that is written correctly for the underlined word.

1 Does you county fair have baking contests? Most fairs have judging for cakes, breads, pies, brownies, and other goodies.

A you's

B your

C you're

D Correct as it is

1 B *Your* refers to the reader. Option A is an incorrect form of a type of pronoun that shows ownership. Option C is a contraction for the words *you are*. Option D is incorrect because *you* cannot show ownership.

Practice

Read the passage. Look at the numbered, underlined portions. Choose the answer that is written correctly for each underlined portion.

Many county fairs hold contests to find the largest vegetables.
(1) At our fair, <u>when</u> is held in September, more than 75 people entered the largest pumpkin judging. You've never seen such huge pumpkins! Some people even needed wheelbarrows to bring
(2) <u>they're</u> entries to the fairgrounds.
(3) The judges weighed each pumpkin carefully. The winner, <u>whose</u> entry weighed 908 pounds, shook hands with the judge. He
(4) grinned proudly. Then he waved <u>their</u> blue ribbon proudly in the air.
(5) The winner, <u>that</u> was a local farmer, made an announcement.
(6) He said he and <u>his</u> wife would make pumpkin pies from <u>my</u> prize-winning pumpkin. They would sell the pies and donate the money to the local homeless shelter.

1
A it
B who
C which
D Correct as it is

2
F their
G them
H there
J Correct as it is

3
A his
B him
C who's
D Correct as it is

4
F him
G there
H his
J Correct as it is

5
A what
B who
C which
D Correct as it is

6
F their
G they
H her
J Correct as it is

Check your answers on page 85.

The noun a pronoun refers to is called its antecedent. The title of this lesson, *Antecedent Agreement*, simply means that the pronoun and the noun are in harmony with each other. On the TABE you'll have to choose correct pronouns that match their antecedents.

Example **Read the sentence. Notice the underlined pronoun *his*. What word does *his* refer to? Draw an arrow from *his* to the word in the first part of the sentence it refers to.**

Randall sometimes forgets to balance <u>his</u> checkbook.

Did you draw the arrow from *his* to *Randall*? The pronoun *his* refers to the noun *Randall*. This sentence needed a pronoun that is singular (Randall is one person), male (Randall is a man), and possessive (Randall owns the checkbook).

Example **Read the sentence. Fill in the blank with the correct possessive pronoun. Then draw an arrow to the pronoun's antecedent.**

Randall's parents drove _____ van to Texas.

Did you write the pronoun *their* and draw a line from *their* to *parents*? In this sentence, the noun to which the plural pronoun refers is *parents*.

Test Example

Read the sentences. Then choose the sentence that is written correctly.

1   A   When Randall's dad was in the U.S. Air Force, he was stationed in Texas.

    B   Randall had never visited Texas, but she hoped to someday.

    C   Randall unfolded a map and found Corpus Christi on them.

    D   Many people take her vacations in warm climates.

---

1   A In this sentence, *he* matches *dad* because they are both singular and male. Option B is not correct because *Randall* is a male, and the pronoun *she* is female. In option C, *them* is plural. It does not agree in number with *map,* which needs the singular pronoun *it*. In option D the singular female pronoun *her* is not correct because the noun *people* needs a plural pronoun.

For numbers 1 through 4, read the paragraph. Look at the numbered, underlined portions. Choose the answer that is written correctly for each underlined portion.

(1)   Keeping on top of <u>her</u> financial situations is a challenge for many Americans. Financial difficulty is a major
(2)   source of stress, and <u>they</u> can strain
(3)   relationships. When <u>they</u> need help, some people turn to credit counseling services. A credit counselor can arrange ways for families and individuals to pay
(4)   <u>your</u> bills.

1
A they
B their
C his
D Correct as it is

2
F he
G she
H it
J Correct as it is

3
A I
B you
C them
D Correct as it is

4
F their
G they're
H his
J Correct as it is

For numbers 5 and 6, read the sentences. Then choose the sentence that is written correctly.

5
A Randall was very happy about his raise at work.
B He called his sister and brother-in-law and told her about it.
C He balanced his checkbook and put them back in the drawer.
D Randall wrote to his parents that he would like to visit him in Texas.

6
F They wrote back that she would love to see him.
G He got his suitcase from the closet and packed them.
H Randall handed him money to the ticket agent at the bus station.
J The bus trip to Corpus Christi was long, but it was also a lot of fun.

Check your answers on page 85.

Lesson 4 · Past Tense

Tense refers to the time when something happens. Is it happening now? Did it happen in the past? Will it happen in the future? To describe something that took place in the past, use the past tense form of a verb. A verb is a word that shows action. On the TABE you will be asked to identify the correct past tense forms of different verbs.

Example **Read the sentence. Notice the underlined verb. When did the action take place?** _____

Last week Robert <u>listened</u> to a great song on the radio.

You probably wrote *last week*. This action took place in the past. Therefore, the verb must be in the past tense. *Listened* is the past tense form of the verb *listen*.

Example **Read the sentence. Underline the two verbs. They are both in the past tense.**

The next day Robert drove to the music store and bought the CD.

Did you underline *drove* and *bought*? Both of these activities took place in the past. *Drove* is the past tense of *drive*. *Bought* is the past tense of *buy*. The chart below gives the correct past tense forms of some common verbs.

Regular verbs		Irregular verbs	
Present tense	**Past tense**	**Present tense**	**Past tense**
listen	listened	drive	drove
arrive	arrived	buy	bought
fill	filled	sit	sat
sign	signed	come	came
complete	completed	take	took

Regular verbs form their past tense by adding *–ed* or *–d* to the end of the verb. Irregular verbs form their past tense by changing spelling.

Test Example

Read the sentences. Then choose the sentence that is written correctly.

1 A The race starts just after we arrived at our seats.

 B The sound of roaring engines filled the night air as we sat down.

 C The checkered flag came down, and the cars take off.

 D The tires squealed as the racing cars bank into the turn.

Language and Spelling

1 B Option B is correct because *filled* is in the past tense. The roaring took place at the same time in the past as when *we sat down*. In option A *starts* is present tense. It should be *started*, the past tense form of this regular verb, because *arrived* is past tense. Option C is incorrect because *take off* is present tense. Option D is incorrect because *squealed* is in the past tense and *bank* is in the present tense, but they should both be in the past tense because they took place at the same time. *Bank* should be *banked*.

Practice

For numbers 1 and 2, read the sentences. Then choose the sentence that is written correctly.

1
A Mark and Rita check the recipe before they went to the grocery store.

B The recipe required coconut milk, which they didn't have at home.

C After they arrived at the store, they ask the clerk for help.

D They look in every aisle until they finally found it.

2
F Alexandra works in a grocery store before she joined the navy.

G She thinks the grocery was OK, but she wanted to study computers.

H After Alexandra joined the navy, she learns about different subjects.

J Her shipmates helped her a lot, and they all became very good friends.

For numbers 3 to 6, read the paragraph. Look at the numbered, underlined portions. Choose the answer that is written correctly for each underlined portion.

(3) One night last week, Mark and Rita <u>decided</u> to make a
(4) Thai dish for dinner. First Mark <u>boiling</u> coconut milk and chili paste in a pot. Then Rita added chicken, lime juice, onions, and
(5) Thai fish sauce. The delicious smells <u>drives</u> them crazy! They
(6) <u>tell</u> all their friends about the wonderful dish.

3
A decides

B decide

C deciding

D Correct as it is

4
F boiled

G boil

H boils

J Correct as it is

5
A drive

B drove

C drived

D Correct as it is

6
F telled

G telling

H told

J Correct as it is

Check your answers on pages 85–86.

Lesson 5 · Future Tense

As you learned in the last lesson, the tense of a verb tells the time of the action. This lesson focuses on using verbs to describe actions that *will take place in the future.* If an action has not yet happened, use the future verb tense.

Example Read the sentence. Notice the underlined verb. When will the action of this verb take place?_____

Dennis <u>will bring</u> his guitar to the party tomorrow night.

Did you write *tomorrow night*? The action will take place tomorrow night. To indicate this, you need to use the future tense of *bring.* To form the future tense of a verb, add *will* before the present tense verb form.

Example Read the sentence. Fill in the blank with the correct future tense form of the verb *start.*

Dennis and Robert _____ a rock group next year. (start)

The correct answer is *will start.* The future tense indicates that the guys plan to start their group at a future time—next year.

Test Example

Read the sentence. Then circle the word or phrase that best completes the sentence.

1 Dennis and Robert _____ some new songs to play at the party next week.

    A learn

    B learning

    C learned

    D will learn

TABE Strategy

Look for clues about time in the sentence, such as *tomorrow night* or *next year,* to indicate that the verb should be future tense.

1 D *Next week* is in the future, so *will learn* is correct. Option A is in the present tense and option C is in the past tense, but the verb needs to be in the future tense. Option B is not correct because it is the *–ing* form of the verb, which is used with *is* or *are* to show continuous action.

For numbers 1 and 2, read the letter. Look at the numbered, underlined portions. Choose the answer that is written correctly for each underlined portion.

Travis Whalin
Manager, The Pulse
456 Nugent Street
Columbus, Ohio 43215

Dear Travis:

My name is Dennis McMahon. I met you last winter at your
(1) club and spoke to you about our band, the Lasers. We recording a
(2) demo tape next week. When it's done, I will send you the tape, along
with some photos and information about our band. After I send
these materials, I will telephone you within 10 days to discuss
playing at your club. Thank you.

Sincerely,

Dennis McMahon

Dennis McMahon

1
A will record
B recorded
C records
D Correct as it is

2
F send
G sended
H sent
J Correct as it is

For numbers 3 and 4, choose the word or phrase that best completes the sentence.

3 Over the coming six months, the Lasers
_____ several hours each week.

A practice
B practiced
C will practice
D were practicing

4 If the Lasers become successful, Dennis
and Robert _____ their day jobs.

F quitted
G quits
H will quit
J quit

Check your answers on page 86.

Lesson 6   Perfect Tense

The perfect tense conveys time relationships. Present perfect tense is formed using the helping verb *has*, or *have*, followed by a past participle. Past perfect tense is formed using the helping verb *had* followed by a past participle. For regular verbs, the past participle is formed by adding *-ed* to the end of the verb. For irregular verbs, the past participle is formed through a change in spelling.

Example **Read the sentence. Did the action of the verb end at a time in the past?**

Or is it continuing into the present? _____

    Mr. and Mrs. Tran have lived in California for ten years.

The action is continuing into the present. This is an example of the present perfect tense. The action began in the past and continues into the present. This sentence uses the plural helping verb *have* because the subject, Mr. and Mrs. Tran, is plural. It also uses the past participle of the regular verb *live, lived*.

Example **Read the sentence. Did the action of the first verb end at a time in the past?**

Or is it continuing into the present? _____

    Mr. Tran had owned a real estate agency before he opened a restaurant.

The action ended at a known time in the past, before Mr. Tran opened a restaurant. This sentence is an example of the past perfect tense. It is used to describe one event following another in the past. The earlier action (had owned) is in the past perfect tense. It uses the helping verb *had* and the past participle of the regular verb *own, owned*. The later action (opened) uses the regular past tense.

Test Example

Read the sentence. Then choose the word or phrase that best completes the sentence.

1 We _____ for many years to buy a house before we finally succeeded last month.

   A have tried

   B had tried

   C try

   D trying

Hint

Sentences with a past perfect verb tense often contain words that show sequence. These include *after*, *before*, *when*, and *as soon as*.

1 **B** *Had tried* shows that the action, *trying to buy a house,* took place before a known time in the past, when *we finally succeeded last month*. Option A indicates that the action of trying to buy a house is completed. Options C *(try)* and D *(trying)* are both in the present tense, which does not show the sequence of events.

For numbers 1 to 4, read the sentence. Then choose the word or phrase that best completes the sentence.

1 I _____ attended the neighborhood block picnic for five years.

A has

B have

C are

D did

2 Our neighbor, Ron Jackson, _____ organized a block picnic five years ago, so he became the planner for our picnic.

F has

G have

H did

J had

3 Ron and his wife Janet _____ printed up a flyer announcing the picnic.

A have

B is

C did

D has

4 One neighbor, Mr. Green, _____ promised to bring a chocolate cake, and I can't wait to taste it.

F had

G have

H has

J did

For numbers 5 and 6, read the sentences. Then choose the sentence that is written correctly.

5 A The organizers of the picnic have all worked very hard.

B The weather report have been promising.

C The Reilly brothers had setting out picnic tables and lawn chairs.

D The preparations have been finished before I got home from work.

6 F When all the food has been placed on the tables, it looked great!

G Over fifty people has been invited, and most came to the picnic.

H By the end of the picnic, everyone had had a terrific time!

J We has hoped to do it all again next summer.

Check your answers on page 86.

Subject and Verb Agreement

Verbs must agree with their subjects. Singular subjects must have singular verbs, and plural subjects must have plural verbs. The TABE will ask you to identify correct forms of verbs that agree with their subjects.

Example **Read the sentence. Notice the underlined verb. Are the subject and verb in this sentence singular or plural?** _____

John, Ravi, and Jolene <u>were</u> all precinct workers in the last election.

The subject and verb are plural. _John, Ravi, and Jolene_ needs the plural verb _were._ When singular subjects are joined by _and_, use a plural verb.

Example **Read the sentence. Underline the verb. Is the verb singular or plural?**

_____

Each day Mary or Karen registers new voters.

Registers is the verb, and it's singular. The subject, _Mary or Karen,_ is also singular. When singular subjects are joined by _or_ or _nor_, use a singular verb.

Example **Read the sentence. Fill in the blank with the verb that best completes the sentence.**

Only one of the city council members _____ an Independent.

Did you write _is?_ The subject of the sentence is _one_, a singular pronoun. Don't be confused by the phrase, _of the city council members_, that follows the subject. Words that come between the subject and the verb do not affect the agreement between the subject and verb.

Test Example

Read the sentence. Then choose the word or phrase that best completes the sentence.

1 The choice of candidates _____ up to the voters.

   A are

   B is

   C were

   D have been

---

1 **B** The subject of this sentence is _choice,_ a singular noun. Therefore the correct answer is _is,_ the singular verb form. The word _candidates_ is plural, but it is not the subject of the sentence. Options A _(are)_, C _(were)_, and D _(have been)_ are all incorrect because they are plural.

For numbers 1 and 2, read the sentence. Then choose the word or phrase that best completes the sentence.

1 The workers _____ at the union hall on Bridge Street.

A are meeting

B is meeting

C meets

D was meeting

2 The owners of the bolt factory _____ a fundraiser for the Republican candidate.

F holds

G is holding

H are holding

J was holding

For numbers 3 and 4, choose the answer that best completes the sentence.

3 Today in the United States, the Republican and Democratic Parties _____ about evenly divided.

A is

B are

C was

D being

4 The Democrats _____ the support of about one-third of the voters. So do the Republicans.

F claims

G is claiming

H claim

J was claiming

For numbers 5 and 6, read the sentences. Then choose the sentence that is written correctly.

5   A Campaign spending was higher than ever.

B Funding for education were a big election issue.

C The voters from Precinct 10 was active lobbyists.

D The local precincts has reported their results.

6   F The school funding referendum have won broad support.

G The city council members were re-elected.

H The ballot boxes is going back into storage until the next election.

J Election Commissioner Bradley have reported the official tally.

Check your answers on pages 86–87.

Many people find certain pairs of verbs confusing. Verbs that sound alike or have similar meanings are often confused. The chart below shows some verb pairs that are often confused.

Verb	Meaning	Verb	Meaning
raise	to lift something up	rise	to stand up, get up, or move oneself up
lay	to put or set something down	lie	to place yourself in a flat position
affect	to influence	effect	to cause to happen or occur
sit	to rest the lower body on a seat	set	to put something down, as on a table
learn	to gain knowledge yourself	teach	to help someone else gain knowledge
leave	to go away from; to drop something off	let	to allow, give permission
accept	to receive; to say yes to	except	to leave out

Example **Read the sentence and the verb choices that follow the sentence. Circle the word that correctly completes the sentence.**

The sign on the door asked all guests to _____ in the chairs along the wall. (sit, set)

In this sentence, *sit* is the right choice. It means to rest yourself on a chair. *Set* means to put down something other than yourself, such as a magazine or a glass. *Be sure to **set** that hot mug of coffee on a coaster* is an example of the word *set* used correctly in a sentence.

Example **Read the sentence and the verb choices that follow the sentence. Circle the word that correctly completes the sentence.**

_____ your hand if you know the answer to the question. (Raise, Rise)

The correct answer is *Raise*. *Raise* means to "lift something up," such as your hand or a flag. *Rise* means to "get up or stand up." It can also mean that an object goes up on its own. You can't "rise" anything other than yourself.

Test Example

Read each sentence. Choose the one that is written correctly.

1 A Elise excepted the job with the county.

   B You can sit your backpack on the kitchen table.

   C To do this job, you have to be able to raise a 50-pound weight over your head.

   D That dog always wants to lay down right in the doorway.

1 C *Raise* means "to lift something up." In this sentence, the job seeker has to be able to lift something (a 50-pound weight) above his or her head. In option A the verb should be *accepted,* which means "to say yes to." In option B, *set* is the right word. It means "to place something." In option D, the verb should be *lie,* not *lay.* The dog wants to place its body in a flat position.

Practice

Read the sentences. Then choose the sentence that is written correctly.

1
A Those fumes from the vat really effected me and gave me a headache.

B How will the layoffs effect your job?

C Sometimes it's hard not to let your mood affect how you do your job.

D The political party is trying to affect a change in the way voters think.

2
F Martin, will you teach me how to boot up the computer?

G A woman from Ford is going to learn us how to write up the agreement.

H Ms. Schmidt is learning the nursing students how to give shots.

J Could you learn me how to operate a drill press?

3
A We had a perfect winning streak, if you accept the rained-out game.

B I'm thinking about excepting the job offer from the newspaper.

C The union has no choice but to except management's offer.

D Did Polly really accept that job looking after the baby chimps at the zoo?

4
F It's important to lay down and rest if you feel sick.

G I'll lay the wrenches on the table and you can choose the one you want.

H The boss asked Helen to lie the envelopes on her desk.

J Ask Scottie to lie those tools on the workbench.

5
A When you are finished with the test, set your pencil down.

B Barney doesn't like to set down during lunch because his back gets stiff.

C Sit that pile of papers on the supervisor's desk.

D Sit your cup on the window ledge and take a look at this!

6
F We rise the flag every morning.

G How early does Lamont have to raise to get to work each morning?

H Rise that handle up about three inches more.

J That spindle will raise automatically when the hole is drilled.

Check your answers on page 87.

Comparative and Superlative Adjectives

Adjectives describe nouns or pronouns. Words you use every day, such as *pretty, red,* and *true,* are adjectives. You will learn about two kinds of adjectives: comparative and superlative. Using adjectives correctly will help make your speaking and writing more colorful.

Examples Read the underlined sentences and circle the adjectives.

Aircraft carriers are large.

Did you circle *large*? *Large* is an adjective that describes *Aircraft carriers.*

An aircraft carrier is larger than a ship.

The correct word to circle is *larger*. *Larger* describes the noun *aircraft carrier.* In this case, *larger* is a comparative adjective. It compares a ship's size with the size of an aircraft carrier.

Rules for Forming and Using Comparative Adjectives
• Use comparative adjectives to compare two people, places, or things. • One-syllable adjectives are made comparative by adding the ending *–er*. • Adjectives with two or more syllables are made comparative by adding the word *more* or *less* before the base adjective.

Sharon is the youngest student in the class.

Did you circle *youngest*? *Youngest* describes the noun *Sharon.* In this case, *youngest* is a superlative adjective. When you compare more than two things, you use the superlative form.

Rules for Forming and Using Superlative Adjectives
• Use superlative adjectives to compare more than two people, places, or things. • One-syllable adjectives are made superlative by adding the ending *–est*. • Adjectives with two or more syllables are made superlative by adding the word *most* or *least* before the base adjective.

See page 99 for a list of comparative and superlative adjectives.

Test Example

Read the sentence. Then choose the word or phrase that best completes the sentence.

1 A badger is _____ than a squirrel.

   A ferociouser

   B ferociousest

   C more ferocious

   D most ferocious

1 C This sentence compares two animals. *Ferocious* is a three-syllable word, so the comparative form is made by adding the word *more*. Option A is an incorrect comparative form. Option B is an incorrect superlative form. This sentence does not call for the superlative form (Option D).

Practice

For numbers 1 through 3, read the paragraph and look at the numbered, underlined portions. Choose the answer that is written correctly for each underlined portion.

(1)   My cousin Dale works at the zoo. Our family visited her last summer. She's a keeper in the African animal exhibit. She finds African animals to be the <u>most appealing</u> of all animals. She especially enjoys working with elephants and hippos. Dale showed us a baby
(2) hippo that had been born the week before. It was <u>cute</u> than an adult hippo. In all, we spent eight hours with
(3) Dale. I wish we could have spent an even <u>long</u> time at the zoo than we did.

1
A appealing
B appealinger
C more appealing
D Correct as it is

2
F cuter   H more cute
G more cuter   J Correct as it is

3
A longest
B more long
C longer
D Correct as it is

For numbers 4 through 6, read the sentence. Then choose the word or phrase that best completes the sentence.

4 Dale thinks that being a zookeeper is the _____ job of all of the jobs in the world.
F fascinating
G more fascinating
H most fascinating
J fascinatinger

5 Dale knows she might have to work _____ hours than in another job.
A longer   C longest
B more long   D long

6 She knows that the job will be _____ than an office job.
F dangerousest   H dangerouser
G most dangerous   J more dangerous

Check your answers on page 87

Adverbs are words that modify verbs and other words. They enhance meaning. Most adverbs can be used to show comparisons. Adverbs answer questions about verbs such as *When did something happen? How did it happen?* or *Where did it happen?* Most, but not all, adverbs end in *–ly*.

Example **Read the sentence and underline the adverb.**

A horse can run swiftly.

Did you underline *swiftly?* You can tell it's an adverb because it answers the question: *How does a horse run?* It describes the action of running.

Example **Read the sentence and underline the adverb.**

Mules work hard.

The adverb in this sentence is *hard.* It answers the question: *How do mules work? Hard* is an adverb that does not end in *–ly*. Other adverbs that do not end in *–ly* include *fair, fast, fine, last, late, once, right, slow, soon, very, well,* and *wrong*.

Example **Read the sentence and underline the adverb.**

Horses run more gracefully than donkeys.

Did you underline *more gracefully?* In this sentence, the gracefulness of two animals is being compared. This calls for a comparative adverb. See the box below for the rules for forming and using comparative adverbs.

Rules for Forming and Using Comparative Adverbs
• Use comparative adverbs to compare two people, places, or things.
• One-syllable adverbs that **do not** end in *–ly* are usually made comparative by adding the ending *–er*.
• Adverbs ending in *–ly* and adverbs with two or more syllables are usually made comparative by adding the word *more* or *less* before the base adjective.

Test Example

Read the sentence. Then choose the word or phrase that best completes the sentence.

1 The trout I caught fought _____ than I expected.

   A most powerfully

   B more powerfully

   C powerfully

   D powerful

1 B Two things are being compared: how powerfully the trout fought and how powerfully the writer *expected* the trout to fight. Therefore, the answer is the correct form of the comparative: *more powerfully*. Option A is incorrect because the sentence is only comparing two things. Option C is not a comparative form. Option D is an adjective, not an adverb.

Practice

For numbers 1 through 4, read the sentence. Then choose the word or phrase that best completes the sentence.

1 To filet that trout, you've got to cut _____ than you're doing.

A more carefully

B most carefully

C carefully

D carefuller

2 We'll have to leave on the fishing trip _____ than we planned.

F more soonly

G soonest

H sooner

J more sooner

3 Eddie caught a trout _____ than John did.

A quickest

B more quicker

C more quickly

D most quickly

4 Penny tried _____ to catch a fish than John did.

F most hard

G harder

H more hard

J most hardest

For numbers 5 and 6, read the sentences. Then choose the sentence that is written correctly.

5

A The breezes in the mountains blew more strongly than at home.

B The breezes in the mountains blew most strongly than at home.

C The breezes in the mountains blew more stronger than at home.

D The breezes in the mountains blew most stronger than at home.

6

F You'll catch a fish most easily in a pond than in a river.

G You'll catch a fish more easily in a pond than in a river.

H You'll catch a fish more easier in a pond than in a river.

J You'll catch a fish more easy in a pond than in a river.

Check your answers on page 87.

Many people confuse adjectives and adverbs. This is because both are modifiers. Modifiers describe words. Adjectives describe nouns or pronouns. Adverbs describe verbs, adjectives, or other adverbs. It is easy to remember that adverbs describe verbs because the word *verb* is part of the word *adverb*. Once you learn a few rules about using these two parts of speech, you will find it much easier to choose the right words.

Example Read the sentence. Then underline the adjective and circle the adverb.

> Mr. Mobley was not in wonderful health, but he still approached life optimistically.

Did you underline *wonderful*? It is an adjective that describes the noun *health*. **The adverb is *optimistically*.** It describes the verb *approached*. Look at the chart on page 99 for an explanation of how adjectives and adverbs are used.

Example Read the sentence and the words in parentheses after the sentence. One of the words in parentheses is an adjective and one is an adverb. Write the correct word in the blank where it belongs.

> Stephen thinks chin-ups are _____, and he did 25 of
> them _____. (easily, easy)

In the first blank, *easy* is the right word. It's an adjective that describes *chin-ups*. **Easily, an adverb, belongs in the second blank.** *Easily* ends in *–ly*, like most adverbs. It answers the question: *How did Stephen do the chin-ups?* He did them easily.

Test Example

Read the sentence and look at the underlined word. Choose the answer that is written correctly for the underlined word.

1 Who is responsible when children do <u>poor</u> in school?

   A poorer

   B poorly

   C more poor

   D Correct as it is

1 B This sentence needs an adverb to describe the verb *do*. Option B is the only adverb among the four choices. Option A is the comparative form of the adjective *poor*. Option C is an incorrect comparative form. Option D is an adjective.

Read the passage. Look at the numbered, underlined portions. Choose the answer that is written correctly for each underlined portion.

(1) Through the years the Olympic Games have provided many <u>glorious</u> memories. Great
(2) athletes have performed <u>mighty</u> before huge crowds. One of the heroes of the 1932 Los Angeles Olympics was Mildred "Babe"
(3) Didrikson. She ran <u>successful</u> in the 80-meter hurdles, winning a <u>gold medal</u>. Didrikson also won the javelin throw, one of the oldest Olympic sports.
    Four years later, the Olympics were held in
(4) Nazi Germany. Sports fans were <u>nervously</u> as the 1936 Games approached. Would Nazi leader
(5) Adolf Hitler greet the U.S. athletes <u>courteously</u>?
(6)   The Americans were led by the <u>magnificently</u> track athlete, Jesse Owens. Owens, an African-
(7) American, won four gold medals. Hitler <u>angry</u> refused to shake Owens' hand. However, Owens became the greatest hero of the Games.

1
A gloriously
B more glorious
C most gloriously
D Correct as it is

2
F mightier
G more mighty
H mightily
J Correct as it is

3
A successfuller
B successfully
C more successful
D Correct as it is

4
F nervous
G more nervously
H nervouser
J Correct as it is

5
A courteous
B more courteous
C more courteously
D Correct as it is

6
F magnificent
G more magnificent
H more magnificently
J Correct as it is

7
A more angry
B more angrily
C angrily
D Correct as it is

Check your answers on page 88.

Negatives are words that express the idea of *no* or *not*. It is always a good idea to use negatives sparingly. To avoid confusion, don't use more than one negative word to express each negative idea. Using negatives correctly will make your writing and speaking easier to understand.

Example **Read the sentence. Underline the negative word.**

> Marshall has never been to Chicago.

Did you underline *never?* It's the only negative word in the sentence. Familiarize yourself with the negative words and negative contractions in the boxes below.

These words are negatives. Use only one of them in a sentence.

no	nothing	never	none
not	no one	nowhere	nobody

These words are negative contractions. Treat them as negatives.

aren't (are not)	can't (cannot)	couldn't (could not)	didn't (did not)
doesn't (does not)	don't (do not)	hasn't (has not)	haven't (have not)
isn't (is not)	wasn't (was not)	weren't (were not)	wouldn't (would not)

Example **Read the sentence. Underline the negative word.**

> I don't care what anyone says!

The correct word to underline is *don't.* It's a contraction for the words *do not* and is a negative.

Example **Write a negative word in the blank.**

> There's _____ anyone can do about the rainy weather.

The word to write is *nothing.* This sentence has just one negative, so it is easy to understand.

Test Example

Read the sentences. Then choose the sentence that is written correctly.

1 A When Sally opened the door, there wasn't nobody there!
   B Frank admitted that the party wasn't any big surprise.
   C Sharice decided she didn't want none of the birthday cake.
   D There isn't nothing he would like better than a new tool kit.

1 B Option B contains only one negative—*wasn't.* Option A is incorrect because it contains two negatives—*wasn't* and *nobody.* Option C also contains two negatives—*didn't* and *none.* Option D also contains two negatives—*isn't* and *nothing.*

For numbers 1 to 4, read the sentences. Then choose the sentence that is written correctly.

1
A My friends and I don't never disagree about where to go dancing.

B There's nothing I enjoy more than dancing.

C Can't nobody get that band to turn down the music?

D Shelley didn't have no coat to wear over her new blouse.

2
F We couldn't find no babysitter for last Saturday.

G Isn't there someone who could look after your daughter while you're away?

H I don't think I'll have none of that apple salad.

J William never says nothing interesting or new.

3
A He didn't think he'd ever get to Tulsa.

B Looking out the bus window, we didn't see nothing but cornfields.

C I don't want to take no long bus trip ever again!

D Ben was angry because there wasn't no one at the station to meet us.

4
F Barbara complained that she didn't never go nowhere.

G No one has ever told us that before!

H Doesn't nobody know what time the bus gets in?

J We won't have no time for dinner before the movie if the bus is late.

For numbers 5 and 6, read the paragraph. Choose the answer that is written correctly for each underlined portion.

(5)   Michael applied for a job with the bus company. He didn't have no experience, but he was very willing to learn. He was also a hard worker, which he felt was in his favor. In addition,
(6)   he hadn't never had any accidents in 15 years of driving. Michael felt sure that the bus company would hire him.

5
A never had no experience

B didn't never have any experience

C didn't have any experience

D Correct as it is

6
F hadn't ever had no accidents

G had never had any accidents

H had never had no accidents

J Correct as it is

Check your answers on page 88.

Choose the word or phrase that best completes the sentence.

1   Her voice sounds _____.

   A badly

   B bad

   C more bad

   D more badly

2   The teachers at the school _____ a fund-raiser every year.

   F hold

   G holds

   H is holding

   J holding

3   _____ is interested in the job at the nursing home.

   A Him

   B Her

   C He

   D Them

4   The racers all _____ at the same time in next week's race.

   F started

   G will start

   H have started

   J starts

Read the sentences. Then choose the sentence that is written correctly.

5   **A** As soon as they saw it, they knew the apartment was perfect.

   B The apartment becomes available just as they started looking.

   C Phillip's family will rent an apartment in that building last week.

   D Would you please sent their mail to the new address after the first of next month?

6   **F** The siren screamed more loud than I had ever heard it.

   G The doctor appeared more sooner than the family expected.

   H The ambulance took Wendy to the hospital fastest than we could.

   J The sick girl's temperature dropped more quickly than the doctor had predicted.

7   **A** A parent needs to be aware of dangers their children face.

   B Young children can get in trouble because of their curiosity.

   C When you bring a household chemical home, put them in a locked cabinet.

   D Household chemicals should be kept in a safe place because it can be dangerous.

8   **F** Please sit the folded flag on the table in the corner.

   G To rise the flag, attach it to the rope with those clips.

   H Students at the technical school raise the flag each morning.

   J My grandfather, a veteran, learned me how to fold a flag correctly.

For numbers 9 through 14, read the paragraph and look at the numbered, underlined portions. Choose the answer that is written correctly for each underlined portion.

(9)   It's hard to imagine a time when American women <u>was</u> not able

(10)   to vote. For more than a century, women <u>didn't have no</u> right to

vote in the United States.

Supporters of voting rights for women were known as

suffragists. They staged protests and hunger strikes. Many of

(11)   <u>them</u> were jailed. However, setbacks only inspired the suffragists

(12)   to struggle <u>more harder</u> for their beliefs. Few women were

(13)   <u>most courageous</u> fighters than Carrie Chapman Catt. Catt had a

plan. She believed that the best way to gain voting rights was to

work in individual states.

In 1920, Congress passed a constitutional amendment that gave

all U.S. women the right to vote in all elections. American women

(14)   had gained <u>them</u> right to cast ballots in any election.

9
  A are
  B were
  C is
  D Correct as it is

10
  F had no
  G never had no
  H hadn't had no
  J Correct as it is

11
  A they
  B we
  C her
  D Correct as it is

12
  F more hardly
  G harder
  H hardest
  J Correct as it is

13
  A more courageously
  B courageous
  C more courageous
  D Correct as it is

14
  F they
  G their
  H her
  J Correct as it is

Check your answers on pages 88–89.

Lesson 13 Sentence Recognition

Knowing how to form sentences is the key to good communication. Sometimes writers forget to include all of the necessary parts of speech or punctuation. This causes run-on sentences or sentence fragments.

How to Recognize a Complete Sentence
• A complete sentence has a subject and a verb.
• It begins with a capital letter and ends with a punctuation mark, such as a
■ period.
■ question mark?
■ exclamation point!

Example **Read the group of words. Is it a complete sentence?**_____

Capital Letter   Verb

My sister needs health insurance.

Subject   Punctuation Mark

Yes. It has a subject and a verb, and it begins with a capital letter and ends with a punctuation mark.

Example **Read the group of words. Is it a complete sentence?**_____

Helped her get health insurance.

No, it is not a complete sentence. Add a subject to correct this fragment: *My father helped her get health insurance.*

How to Recognize a Sentence Fragment
• Sentences that are missing either a subject or a verb—or both—are called sentence fragments.
• Sentence fragments do not express complete thoughts.
How to Correct a Sentence Fragment
• If there is no subject, add one.
• If there is no verb, add one.
• If there is a partial verb, complete it.
• If the sentence does not express a complete thought, complete it.

Example **Read this run-on sentence. How can you make it two sentences?**_____

_____

I hope the baby isn't sick it takes all day to go to the doctor's office.

There should be a period after the word *sick*. The word *it* should be capitalized.

Read the sentences. Then choose the sentence that is written correctly.

1   A   A decent health care benefits package.

    B   Considering taking a job with the county.

    C   Premiums have gone up I need to look for a new plan.

    D   Many employers have cut back on health insurance benefits.

Hint

If you can't tell *who* or *what* is doing the action or *what* the action is, it's probably a sentence fragment.

1   D   This sentence has both a subject *(employers)* and a verb *(have cut back)*. It also begins with a capital letter and ends with a period. Option A lacks a verb. Option B lacks a subject. Option C is a run-on sentence.

Practice

For numbers 1 and 2, read the sentences. Then choose the sentence that is written correctly.

1   A Choosing a family doctor.

    B The family doctor they chose.

    C Melinda and Paul chose a family doctor.

    D They chose a new doctor she's from Pakistan.

2   F One of their children was born deaf.

    G They have two children one is only four months old.

    H Are interested in baby care.

    J Paul's father, who used a wheelchair.

For numbers 3 and 4, read the paragraph and look at the numbered, underlined portions. Choose the answer that is written correctly for each underlined portion.

(3)   The emergency room was very <u>crowded. When</u> Paul and Melinda
(4)   arrived. <u>They breathed a sigh of relief when the nurse called their name.</u>

3   A crowded. when

    B Crowded. when

    C crowded when

    D Correct as it is

4   F They breathed a sigh of relief. When the nurse called their name.

    G They breathing a sigh of relief when the nurse called their name.

    H They breathed a sigh of relief the nurse called their name.

    J Correct as it is

Check your answers on page 89.

Lesson 14 Adding Modifiers to Combine Sentences

Modifiers are words and phrases you can add to sentences. Adding modifiers will help you avoid writing short, choppy, repetitive sentences. Modifiers turn simple sentences into more specific ones. Once you know how to use modifiers, your writing will be more interesting.

Example **Read these sentences. Write a sentence that combines the information from both sentences.** _____

    Sentence 1   John has a new puppy.
    Sentence 2   The puppy is brown.

The combined sentence is: John has a new brown puppy. This sentence is best combined by moving the adjective *brown* from Sentence 2 into Sentence 1.

Example **Read these sentences. Then combine them into one sentence.** _____

    Sentence 1   The horse ran across the finish line.
    Sentence 2   The horse ran swiftly.
    Sentence 3   The horse ran gracefully.

The combined sentence is: The horse ran swiftly and gracefully across the finish line. This sentence is best combined by joining the adverbs from Sentences 2 and 3 into a phrase using the conjunction *and,* and then inserting the phrase into Sentence 1.

Example **Read these sentences. Then combine them into one sentence.** _____

    Sentence 1   The audience applauded as the firefighters entered.
    Sentence 2   The audience applauded loudly.
    Sentence 3   The firefighters were heroic.

The combined sentence is: The audience applauded loudly as the heroic firefighters entered. This sentence is best combined by moving the adverb *loudly* from Sentence 2 and the adjective *heroic* from Sentence 3 into Sentence 1.

Test Example

Read the underlined sentences. Then circle the letter of the sentence that best combines those sentences into one.

  1   Maria bought a new car today.

      The car is fast.

      A   Maria bought a new fast car today.

      B   Today Maria bought a new car that is fast.

      C   The car that Maria bought today is new and fast.

      D   Maria bought a new and fast car.

Practice

For numbers 1 through 4, read the underlined sentences. Choose which answer best combines the sentences into one.

1 The Marines marched in the parade.

The Marines marched proudly.

The Marines marched expertly.

A The Marines marched proudly and they marched expertly in the parade.

B In the parade, the Marines marched proudly and expertly.

C The Marines marched proudly and expertly in the parade.

D The Marines marched proudly and expertly.

2 Malcolm visited his job counselor yesterday.

Malcolm's job counselor was named Lisa.

F Yesterday, Malcolm visited Lisa, his job counselor.

G Yesterday, Malcolm visited Lisa, Malcolm's job counselor.

H Malcolm visited Lisa, his job counselor and he visited her yesterday.

J Malcolm visited his job counselor yesterday, and his job counselor's name was Lisa.

3 The trees were tall and beautiful.

The trees were cut down to make room for the highway.

A The tall and beautiful trees were cut down.

B The tall, beautiful trees were cut down to make room for the highway.

C The trees were tall, beautiful trees, and they were cut down to make room for the highway.

D The trees were tall and beautiful, and the trees were cut down to make room for the highway.

4 I screamed when I saw a snake on the trail this morning.

The snake was big.

I screamed loudly.

F I screamed when I saw a big snake on the trail this morning.

G I screamed loudly when I saw a big snake on the trail this morning.

H I screamed loudly when I saw a snake on the trail this morning.

J When I saw a big snake on the trail, I screamed loudly.

Check your answers on page 89.

Lesson 15 Compounding

Good writers avoid using short, choppy sentences because they tend to sound repetitive and dull. Combining or compounding sentences is key to good writing. The TABE asks you to combine pairs of short, related sentences. If the verbs of both sentences are similar, you can combine the subjects with the word *and*.

Example **Read these two sentences and the combined sentence. How are they combined into one sentence?**

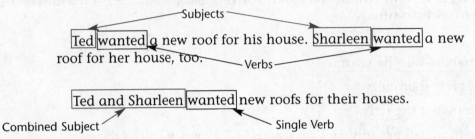

Ted wanted a new roof for his house. Sharleen wanted a new roof for her house, too.

Ted and Sharleen wanted new roofs for their houses.

Combined Subject   Single Verb

Ted and Sharleen are combined with **and** to form a combined subject. The verb in both sentences is **wanted,** so the verb is stated just once.

Example **Here are two more short sentences. Try combining them by joining the subjects.** _____

Angela got a home-improvement loan. Charlie got one, too.

You probably wrote something like this: Angela and Charlie got home-improvement loans. You joined the subjects and stated the verb once. You have combined two short, choppy sentences into one that is easier to read.

Test Example

Read the underlined sentences. Then choose the answer that best combines those sentences into one.

Most homes qualify for low-interest loans.

Many larger structures also qualify for low-interest loans.

1 A Most homes with larger structures qualify for low-interest loans.

B Most homes and many larger structures qualify for low-interest loans.

C Most homes qualify and many larger structures qualify for low-interest loans.

D Most homes qualify for low-interest loans, and many larger structures also qualify for low-interest loans.

TABE **Strategy**

Read test directions carefully. The word *best* is an important clue in these directions.

1 B This sentence combines the subjects and states the verb once. Option A changes the meaning of the two sentences. Option C repeats *qualify*. Option D repeats *qualify for low-interest loans.*

Practice

Read the underlined sentences. Then choose the answer that best combines those sentences into one.

1 Charlie filled out an application for a home-improvement loan.

His neighbor filled out an application, too.

A Charlie and his neighbor filled out applications for home-improvement loans.

B Charlie filled out an application for a home-improvement loan, along with his neighbor.

C Charlie filled out and his neighbor filled out applications for home-improvement loans.

D Charlie filled out an application for a home-improvement loan, and his neighbor filled out an application, too.

2 The front of the form had to be completed.

The back of the form also had to be completed.

F The front and the back had to be completed.

G The front and the back of the form had to be completed.

H The front of the form and the back of the form had to be completed.

J The front of the form had to be completed, and the back of the form had to be completed.

3 Contractors can install new doors and windows.

Dealers can install new doors and windows, too.

A Contractors can install new doors, windows, and dealers.

B Contractors and dealers can install new doors and windows.

C Contractors can work with dealers to install new doors and windows.

D Contractors can install new doors and windows, and dealers can also install new doors and windows.

4 A little planning can make a big difference in your house.

A small loan can help make a big difference in your house.

F A little planning and a small loan can make a big difference in your house.

G A little planning in your house and a small loan can help make a big difference.

H A little planning can make a big difference, and a small loan can help your house.

J A little planning can make a big difference in your house, and a small loan can help make a big difference.

Check your answers on page 90.

Lesson 16 Coordinating

Coordinating conjunctions like *and, but,* and *or* are used to connect parts of sentences. They can help you avoid short, choppy sentences.

Example Read the two sentences. Each contains some information. In the sentence below them, the information from both sentences is combined into a single sentence joined by the conjunction *and*.

Sentence 1	Stan likes to read.
Sentence 2	Wanda likes to play the piano.
Combined Sentence	Stan likes to read, and Wanda likes to play the piano.

From Sentence 1   Coordinating Conjunction   From Sentence 2

When joining two sentences like this, you usually place a comma after the first part.

Example Here's another example. What word does the combined sentence use to link the two sentences?_____

Sentence 1	Dogs make great pets.
Sentence 2	Cougars do not make great pets.
Combined Sentence	Dogs make great pets, but cougars do not.

In the combined sentence, the information is joined using the word *but.* Did you notice that the combined sentence does not include the words *make great pets* from the second sentence? These words are not needed because they repeat words from the first sentence.

Test Example

Read the underlined sentences. Then circle the letter of the sentence that best combines the sentences into one.

1 Molly wanted to swim in the ocean.

   Swimming in the ocean was too dangerous.

   A The ocean was too dangerous to swim in, Molly wanted to swim in the ocean.

   B The ocean was too dangerous for Molly, but Molly wanted to swim in it.

   C Molly wanted to swim in the ocean, but it was too dangerous.

   D Molly wanted to swim in the dangerous ocean.

1 C This choice best combines all the information from both of the sentences without repeating or leaving out any information. *But* joins the sentences, and *it* is used to avoid repeating *swimming in the ocean.* In option A, *the ocean* and *swim in* are repeated. *But* is omitted, making the sentence a run-on. In option B, *Molly* is repeated. In option D, *but* is left out and so is the detail that the ocean is *too dangerous* to swim in.

For numbers 1 through 6, read the underlined sentences. Then circle the letter of the sentence that best combines those sentences into one.

1 Many people like rock music.

Other people prefer country music.

A Many other people like rock and country.

B Many people like rock music, but others prefer country.

C Many people and other people like rock and country music.

D Many people like rock music, and other people like country music, too.

2 I like cooking hamburgers on a grill.

It's not messy at all with a gas grill.

F Cooking hamburgers on a grill is not messy at all with a gas grill.

G I like cooking hamburgers on a grill, it's not messy at all with a gas grill.

H I like cooking hamburgers on a grill, and it's not messy at all with a gas grill.

J It's not messy at all with a gas grill, and I like cooking hamburgers on a grill.

3 I asked the mail carrier to leave the mail in the box.

The mail carrier left it on the porch bench.

A The mail carrier left the mail on the porch bench, but I asked her to leave the mail in the box.

B I asked the mail carrier to leave the mail in the box, but the mail carrier left it on the porch bench.

C I asked the mail carrier to leave the mail in the box, but she left it on the porch bench.

D I asked the mail carrier to leave the mail in the box on the porch bench.

4 The teachers at our school enjoy teaching.

The students at our school can certainly tell that the teachers enjoy teaching.

F The teachers at our school enjoy teaching, and the students can certainly tell that the teachers enjoy teaching.

G The teachers at our school enjoy teaching, and the students at our school can certainly tell.

H The teachers at our school enjoy teaching, and the students can certainly tell.

J The teachers and the students at our school enjoy teaching.

5 Eleanor locked the door when she left.

The burglars got in anyway.

A Eleanor locked the door when she left, but the burglars got in anyway.

B The burglars got in anyway, but Eleanor locked the door when she left.

C Eleanor locked the door, but the burglars got in when she left anyway.

D Eleanor locked the door when she left, the burglars got in anyway.

6 Hundreds of people attended the show.

They definitely got their money's worth!

F Hundreds of people attended the show, they definitely got their money's worth!

G Hundreds of people attended the show, and they definitely got their money's worth!

H Hundreds of people attended the show, hundreds of people definitely got their money's worth!

J Hundreds of people attended the show, and they definitely got their money's worth from the show!

Check your answers on page 90.

When you read a sentence and can't tell what word describes what, the problem is usually a misplaced modifier. A **modifier** is a word or phrase that limits, or adds to the meaning of, another word or phrase used with it. *Where* you place a modifier makes a very big difference in the meaning of a sentence. A misplaced modifier can completely change the meaning of a sentence. As a rule, you should always put modifiers next to the words they describe.

Example **Read the sentence and notice the underlined words. Do the underlined words modify *poodle* or *woman*?** _____

I saw a woman walking a poodle <u>with a baseball cap</u>.

The underlined words incorrectly modify *poodle*, making it sound like the poodle was wearing a baseball cap. The writer probably intended to say that the woman was wearing the hat, like this: *I saw a woman wearing a baseball cap walking a poodle.*

Example **Read the sentence and notice the underlined word. What does the underlined word modify?**_____

Terri <u>almost</u> spent a thousand dollars on car repairs.

The word *almost* modifies *spent*. This is a misplaced modifier. As written, the meaning is: *Terri almost spent the money, but then for some reason she didn't.* The writer meant to say that the amount Terri spent on her car was close to a thousand dollars. Misplaced modifiers can be corrected by changing the word order. The sentence should read:

Terri spent <u>almost</u> a thousand dollars on car repairs.

When *almost* is closer to *a thousand dollars,* the meaning is clear: Terri's repair bill was close to a thousand dollars.

Test Example

Read the sentence and look at the underlined portion. Choose the answer that is written correctly for the underlined portion.

1 We put the salad <u>in the refrigerator, we planned to eat it the next day</u>.

   A in the refrigerator, which we planned to eat the next day.

   B , which we planned to eat the next day, in the refrigerator.

   C that we planned to eat the next day, we put the salad in the refrigerator.

   D Correct as it is

1 **B** In option A, the meaning is that they are planning to eat the refrigerator. Option C is a run-on sentence that repeats many words. Option D is a run-on sentence. It's also unclear whether *it* refers to the salad or the refrigerator.

For numbers 1 to 6, read the passage and look at the numbered, underlined portions. Circle the letter of the sentence that is written correctly for each underlined portion.

(1)   At the age of 12, Jenny's dad remarried. My wife and I were invited to the wedding. It was
(2) held on a cold day in November. Falling gently outside the window, we could see the first snowflakes of the year. The church was lit entirely with candles. Guests from all around
(3) the state attended the wedding. A soloist with a beautiful voice sang a few songs.
    After the wedding, the reception was held at a
(4) local restaurant. Walking past the food table, the wedding cake looked delicious! I had three pieces
(5) and could have eaten more. A band provided music for dancing with a great saxophone player. Some kids were teaching us older people some new dances. They were wild, but fun! My wife
(6) and I almost stayed at the reception until midnight. We didn't get home until quarter of one. As you can guess, we had a terrific time!

1
A Jenny was 12, her dad remarried.

B When Jenny was 12, her dad remarried.

C When he was 12, Jenny's dad remarried.

D Correct as it is

2
F We could see the first snowflakes of the year falling gently outside the window.

G We, falling gently outside the window, could see the first snowflakes of the year.

H We could see the first snowflakes, falling gently outside the window, of the year.

J Correct as it is

3
A sang with a beautiful voice. A few songs.

B sang a few songs with a beautiful voice.

C with a beautiful voice. Sang a few songs.

D Correct as it is

4
F The wedding cake looked delicious walking past the food table!

G We saw the wedding cake walking past the food table, and it looked delicious!

H We saw the wedding cake as we were walking past the food table, and it looked delicious!

J Correct as it is

5
A with a great saxophone player provided music for dancing.

B provided music with a great saxophone player for dancing.

C provided music for dancing. With a great saxophone player.

D Correct as it is

6
F stayed almost at the reception until midnight.

G stayed at the reception until almost midnight.

H stayed at the reception almost until midnight.

J Correct as it is

Check your answers on page 90.

Lesson 18 Nonparallel Structure

In writing, **parallel structure** means that similar parts of sentences are expressed in a like way. Using the same pattern of words shows that two or more ideas have the same importance. Parallel structures are usually joined with coordinating conjunctions, such as *and*. The TABE will ask you to recognize whether sentences have parallel structure.

Example **Read the two sentences. The sentence marked *Incorrect* does not have parallel structure. The sentence marked *Correct* does have parallel**

structure. What is similar about the correct sentence? _____

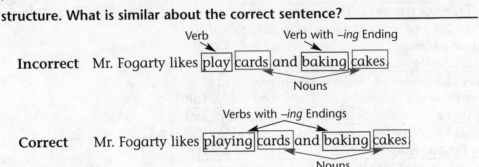

In the correct sentence, the two things Mr. Fogarty likes both have a verb with an *–ing* ending (*playing* and *baking*) and a noun *(cards and cakes)*. In the incorrect sentence, the verbs have different forms. One is a regular verb and the other is a verb with an *–ing* ending.

Example **Read the sentence. Then fill in the blank with words that have the same form as *snapping his fingers*.**

The stranger walked down the street snapping his fingers and _____

_____ .

You may have written something like *whistling a tune* or *shuffling his feet*. Your answer should start with an *–ing* verb.

Test Example

Read the sentence and look at the underlined portion. Choose the answer that is written correctly for the underlined portion.

1 Our family likes <u>to bicycle, canoe, and camping.</u>

   A to bicycle, canoeing, and camp.

   B bicycling, canoeing, and camping.

   C to bicycle, go canoeing, and camping.

   D bicycling, canoeing, and when we go camping.

---

1 B The three things the family likes to do all end in an *–ing* verb. In option A, *bicycle* and *camp* are in the same form, but *canoeing* is not. In option C, *camping* does not have the same form as *to bicycle* and *go canoeing*. In option D, *bicycling* and *canoeing* are in the same form, but *when we go camping* is in a different form.

For numbers 1 to 6, read the passage and look at the numbered, underlined portions. Circle the letter of the sentence that is written correctly for each underlined portion.

(1) A terrible fire had destroyed the church. Only a few burned walls were left standing. The members of the church decided <u>tearing down and rebuilding the church was the only solution</u>. It would have cost too much to try to repair it.

(2) So, on a lovely spring day, the members and their friends went to work. Even young children seemed to enjoy <u>to help the adults and lending a hand</u>. Some members of the church had special skills, but

(3) most did not. People began <u>measuring with rulers and cut wood</u> for the frame. Others were busy

(4) <u>sawing, hammer, and picking up trash around the building site</u>. Still other church members spent

(5) their time <u>fixing food and when they bring snacks and drinks to the workers</u>. Everyone in the big crowd was excited.

It took several weeks to rebuild the church, even with dozens of people working on the project.

(6) However, by summer, the members were happy <u>to be once again sing and praying in their own</u> church.

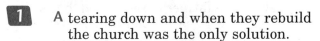

1
A tearing down and when they rebuild the church was the only solution.

B tearing down and to rebuild the church was the only solution.

C to tear down and rebuilding the church was the only solution.

D Correct as it is

2
F helping the adults and lend a hand.

G helping the adults and lending a hand.

H when they help the adults and lending a hand.

J Correct as it is

3
A measuring with rulers and cutting wood

B measuring with rulers and to cut wood

C to measure with rulers and cutting wood

D Correct as it is

4
F to sawing, hammering, and picking up trash around the building site.

G sawing, hammering, and picking up trash around the building site.

H to saw, hammer, and picking up trash around the building site.

J Correct as it is

5
A fixing food and bring snacks and drinks to the workers.

B to fix food and bringing snacks and drinks to the workers.

C fixing food and bringing snacks and drinks to the workers.

D Correct as it is

6
F to be once again singing and when they pray

G to be once again singing and praying

H to be once again singing and pray

J Correct as it is

Check your answers on pages 90–91.

Read the sentences. Circle the letter of the sentence that is written correctly.

1

   A Saving a lot of money.

   B Not have to go to the store.

   C A yearly subscription to that magazine.

   D You receive it on the first of each month.

For numbers 2 through 4 circle the letter of the sentence that best combines those sentences into one.

2

The barn is 120 feet long.

The barn is red.

   F The red barn is 120 feet long.

   G The barn is red and is 120 feet long.

   H The barn is red and it is 120 feet long.

   J The barn is 120 feet long, and it is red.

3

Farming is an important business in our area.

Mining is an important business in our area.

   A Farming is an important business in our area, and mining is an important business in our area.

   B Farming is an important business in our area, mining is an important business in our area.

   C Farming and mining is an important business in our area.

   D Farming and mining are important businesses in our area.

4

Farmers are usually very careful.

Some are injured on the job.

   F Farmers are usually very careful, but some are injured on the job.

   G Some are injured on the job but farmers are usually very careful.

   H Some farmers are injured, but some are very careful on the job.

   J Farmers are usually very careful, some are injured on the job.

Read the paragraph and look at the numbered, underlined portions. Circle the letter of the sentence that is written correctly for each underlined portion.

(5)   All the farmers I know enjoy working outdoors and when they

(6)   can be their own boss. Looking out over their fields sitting on a

tractor, farmers feel great satisfaction.

5

   A working outdoors and to be their own boss.

   B to work outdoors and being their own boss.

   C working outdoors and being their own boss.

   D Correct as it is

6

   F Farmers, sitting on their tractors and looking out over their fields, feel great satisfaction.

   G Sitting looking out over their fields on a tractor, farmers feel great satisfaction.

   H Farmers feel great satisfaction looking out over their fields sitting on their tractors.

   J Correct as it is

Check your answers on page 91.

Lesson 19 Topic Sentence

A paragraph is a group of sentences that develop a single topic, or subject. The topic sentence presents the topic of a paragraph. It usually comes at the beginning of a paragraph. At work and at home, writing well-organized paragraphs will help you communicate better with others.

Example Read the paragraph. The topic sentence is underlined.

> Knowing a foreign language is valuable in many ways. It can help you take part in international business and broaden your career horizons. It can also help you to better understand foreign cultures. Finally, understanding and appreciating foreign languages will help you to understand and appreciate your own native language.

In this paragraph, everything that follows the topic sentence gives more information about it. Each sentence tells why the writer believes that knowing a foreign language is valuable in many ways.

Example Read the paragraph. Write a topic sentence in the blank line at the beginning of the paragraph.

> _____. In 1900, airplanes had not yet flown into the sky. There were only a few cars on a few roads. Horses and buggies could be seen everywhere. Trains were common, but space travel was just a dream of science fiction writers. What a difference 100 years can make!

You probably wrote something like *Transportation has changed a lot over the last 100 years.* A topic sentence like this introduces the subject of the paragraph. It lets the reader know what to expect in the rest of the paragraph.

Test Example

Read the paragraph. Then circle the letter of the topic sentence that best fills the blank in the paragraph.

1 _____. Your spot should be quiet, well lit, and comfortable. Have everything you need, such as pencils and paper, close at hand. Ask friends and family not to bother you. Turn off the TV and radio.

A Studying is easier when you have a good place to study.

B Some people prefer pens, while others like pencils.

C You may need a 100-watt bulb in your study lamp.

D Good grades will help you get a better job.

Hint

When writing a topic sentence, write a general statement that focuses on the main subject of the paragraph.

1 **A** Option A sums up the rest of the details in the paragraph. Option B is a true statement, but it has nothing to do with what makes a good study place. Option C is not a topic sentence. It is a detail. Option D, while true, does not introduce the topic of a good place to study.

Practice

For numbers 1 through 4, read the paragraph. Then circle the letter of the topic sentence that best fills the blank in the paragraph.

1 _____. First, they supply us with wool. Wool is a terrific fiber for high-quality, warm clothing. Sheep also give us lamb, a delicious meat. Sheep improve the land they graze on. Finally, other sheep products, such as lanolin, help make our lives better.

A Sheep are very valuable animals.

B Some people don't like the taste of lamb.

C Sheep are among the most misunderstood animals.

D You'll love a warm wool sweater on a cold winter day.

2 _____. It's a very fast game. Players zip up and down the court at incredible speeds. It also takes amazing skill. The best players are unbelievable athletes. We can admire their abilities—even if we could never do the things these men and women do!

F Michael Jordan was a better basketball player than Magic Johnson ever was!

G Why has basketball become more popular than baseball?

H We admire the skills of professional basketball players.

J Why is basketball such a popular sport?

3 _____. In English and the Scandinavian languages, there are names like John*son* and Ander*son*. In Russian names, the *–vitch* or *–vich* endings mean "son of." In Irish names, such as O'Riley and O'Malley, the *O'* means the same. Do you known anyone named MacDonald or MacArthur? *Mac* is used in Scottish names for— you guessed it—son of!

A Studying names from different languages is interesting.

B Parents sometimes treat sons differently from daughters.

C Names that mean "son of" exist in many different languages.

D Many parents choose to name their children after family members.

4 _____. To the north, there is Canada. Founded by the British and French, Canada is huge, lightly populated, and cold. The Spanish settled Mexico, our southern neighbor. It is also a large country, but its population is much larger than Canada's. Mexico is also much warmer. Much of its climate is tropical.

F Canada is a better country than Mexico or the United States.

G Our two closest neighbors are very different.

H Warm climates are healthier than cold ones.

J Parts of Canada are French-speaking.

Check your answers on page 91.

Lesson 20 Supporting Sentences

In a paragraph, good writers use supporting sentences to provide details about the topic sentence. The TABE will ask you to choose supporting sentences that best develop a topic sentence.

Example Read the paragraph. The topic sentence is underlined. What kind of information is contained in the supporting sentences that follow it?_____

_____

Memorial Park contains many different kinds of trees. Among the most impressive are the stately oaks along the main path. Along the river are some beautiful sycamores with their unusual bark.

Each sentence following the topic sentence gives information about the different kinds of trees in the park. Supporting sentences offer details related to the topic sentence.

Example Read the topic sentence. On the line following the topic sentence, write one supporting sentence that gives details about the topic sentence.

There are so many things I dislike about city traffic! _____

_____

You probably wrote something like *I really dislike how slow drivers clog up the fast lane on the freeway* or *I wish drivers would use their turn signals.* For this topic sentence, you should have written an example of something you don't like about traffic.

Test Example

Read the topic sentence. Then circle the letter of the answer that best develops the topic sentence.

1 Staying at home with my family is more fun than going out.

   A I have three kids, two girls and a boy. The oldest girl is really sharp. She helps me take care of the other kids. Even though she's only 11, she is a great help.

   B I get to spend time with my kids, reading them stories, and playing games and watching TV with them. It's a lot cheaper, it's a lot more interesting, and it's less stressful. Plus, I don't have to worry about driving.

   C Our family is thinking about moving to a new apartment. The one we're in now just isn't big enough. I'm trying to save money by staying home.

   D The last time I went out, I nearly had an accident. The roads were icy. Some crazy driver missed my car by half an inch. If I had wrecked my car, I don't know what I would have done.

Practice

Circle the letter of the answer that best develops the topic sentence.

1 Cesar Chavez is an American hero.

A Like Martin Luther King, Jr., Chavez believed in nonviolent protest. King gained national attention for his leadership of the Montgomery bus boycott. King went on to lead other protests, and he won the Nobel Peace Prize.

B His goal was to improve the lives of America's migrant workers. Chavez formed a farm workers' union in 1962. After many years, they finally won a union contract and a hope for better lives.

C Farm workers often worked for five dollars a day under very bad conditions. Workdays often stretched to 16 hours under a broiling sun.

D Mexican Americans have made many important contributions to U.S. society and culture. Music, food, literature, and politics are just a few of the many areas to which Mexican Americans have contributed.

2 Working a night shift can be a good arrangement for some people.

F Getting to work a little early is a good idea. That way you can take care of things and still be at the job when it starts.

G Scientists say that working at night can disturb body rhythms in some people. Among the problems are sleeplessness, lack of appetite, and vision difficulties.

H There are a number of benefits. You can shop and do errands during off-peak hours. Sometimes, the pay is higher if you work at night.

J Some kinds of jobs in which night-shift work is common are factory, retail, customer service, and transportation.

3 Saving for retirement is a big challenge.

A For many people, Social Security alone will not provide enough money. These people may have to work longer than they had planned.

B Checking accounts usually pay no interest at all. They are good for paying bills. However, they are not really a long-term savings plan.

C Finding the time to start a savings plan is difficult, especially for single parents. There's work, looking after the kids, and doing all the shopping. That leaves very little time left over for talking to banks.

D In some countries, every worker receives a government pension. Individual retirement savings plans are rare.

Check your answers on pages 91–92.

Supporting sentences in a paragraph need to be in the correct order. If your sentences are in the wrong order your readers will be confused. You can't explain which horse won the race before you mention the horse race. The TABE will ask you to place sentences in their correct order in a paragraph.

Example **Read the paragraph. Notice how the sentences are arranged in a logical order, starting with the topic sentence.**

> Walter decided that he finally had to do something about the termites in his house. He got out the telephone book. He called the number of an exterminator and made an appointment. When he hung up the phone, he felt better.

Sequence of Events
1. Walter decided to do something about the termites.
2. Walter used a phone book to find an exterminator.
3. Walter called the exterminator and made an appointment.
4. Walter hung up the phone and felt better.

In the topic sentence of this paragraph, you learn about Walter's decision to do something about his termite problem. The rest of the paragraph describes what he did, *in the order that he did it*. If you were to change the sequence of events, the paragraph would not make sense.

Example **In the following paragraph, one of the sentences is in the wrong place. Circle the sentence that is out of place. Then draw an arrow to where you think it should be.**

> Evelyn decided to go on a picnic. She packed a lunch. After unpacking and eating her lunch, Evelyn sat on the grass. She drove to a park near where she lived. "What a great spring day!" she thought.

The sentence that is out of place is *She drove to a park near where she lived.* It should come before *After unpacking and eating her lunch, Evelyn sat on the grass.*

Test Example

Read the paragraph. Then circle the letter of the sentence that best fills in the blank in the paragraph.

1 Hafez ran from his car to the front porch. He took out his key. _____ Then Hafez took off his wet coat and hung it on the hook.

 A He was late getting home.

 B He took off his hat and gloves.

 C He heard the telephone ringing.

 D He opened the front door and went in.

1 **D** The paragraph needs a sentence to tell you that Hafez went inside. It happened *after* he took out his key and *before* he took off his coat. Options A, B, and C might all be true statements. However, they do not tell you what happened *after* he took out his key and *before* he took off his coat.

Practice

For numbers 1 to 4, circle the letter of the sentence that best fills the blank in the paragraph.

1 The coach was very unhappy with the way her team was playing. When one player missed an easy shot, the coach had seen enough. _____ The players sat down on the bench. Then the coach lectured them in an angry voice.

A The fans started booing loudly.

B The team had lost an 11-point lead.

C The coach angrily kicked a chair leg.

D She signaled to the referee for a timeout, and called the team to the sideline.

2 Britney and Samantha were very excited about trick-or-treating on Halloween. They got dressed in their costumes. _____ When they got home, they dumped all their candy on the floor.

F Each child picked out her own costume.

G They went to bed soon after coming home.

H It's not surprising that both had stomachaches!

J They went from door to door in the neighborhood.

3 Making popcorn on the stove is easy. Pour the oil in the pan and heat it up. _____ When the corn starts to pop, shake the pan to avoid burning the corn.

A Turn on the stove.

B Buy the popcorn.

C Put the popcorn in the pan and place the lid on the pan.

D Be careful using the stove.

4 As it neared the horizon, the sun turned a fiery orange. Clouds in the western sky became pink and red. Just before the sun sank out of sight, it turned bright red. _____ The countryside grew dark quickly.

F Then the sun disappeared.

G Shadows began to grow longer.

H Not a light could be seen anywhere.

J The sun started to go down about 6:00.

Check your answers on page 92.

Lesson 22 Unrelated Sentences

All the supporting sentences in a paragraph must relate directly to the topic sentence. Supporting sentences can give details or examples. They can compare and contrast. No matter how they do it, every sentence in a paragraph needs to be about the subject of the paragraph. The TABE will ask you to select sentences that do *not* belong in paragraphs.

Example **Read the paragraph. The underlined sentence does not belong in the paragraph. Can you explain why?** _____

> My brother's a plumber and my sister is a carpenter. They have worked together on many jobs. <u>Women carpenters are fairly unusual.</u> They also do jobs for my husband and me—very convenient!

This sentence does not belong because it is a general statement that is unrelated to the main topic. The main topic is the writer's brother and sister.

Example **Read the paragraph. Underline the sentence that does not belong in the paragraph.**

> Some people think there's nothing better than riding a roller coaster. Roller coasters can be made of wood or steel. Roller coaster fans travel from amusement park to amusement park. They like to "collect" coaster rides the way some people collect stamps!

You should have underlined *Roller coasters can be made of wood or steel.* This sentence does not fit because the other three sentences are about roller coaster fans. The sentence gives true but unrelated information about roller coasters themselves.

Test Example

Read the paragraph. Then circle the letter of the sentence that does not belong in the paragraph.

1 1. Watching birds at a backyard or window feeder can be fascinating. 2. Hunting and fishing are also popular outdoor hobbies. 3. In wintertime, birds will flock to a feeder in large numbers. 4. You can see as many as ten different types of birds at the feeder at once.

Hint

Read the paragraph four times, each time leaving out a sentence. It will read smoothly without the unrelated sentence.

   A Sentence 1

   B Sentence 2

   C Sentence 3

   D Sentence 4

1 B Sentence 2 is about other outdoor hobbies, so it does not belong in the paragraph. Options A, C, and D belong because they focus on the main topic, backyard bird feeders.

Read the paragraph. Then circle the letter of the sentence that does not belong in the paragraph.

1 1. The Pilgrims, who came to Massachusetts in 1620, started the Thanksgiving holiday. 2. Many of the Pilgrims had spent time in Holland before coming to America. 3. They had a hard first winter and many people died. 4. However, the second year was better, and they gathered for a meal to give thanks.

A Sentence 1

B Sentence 2

C Sentence 3

D Sentence 4

2 1. Justin was very excited when his father brought home the computer. 2. They worked together to set it up in the bedroom. 3. Justin's parents had been divorced for three years. 4. Justin's face lit up when they turned it on for the first time.

F Sentence 1

G Sentence 2

H Sentence 3

J Sentence 4

3 1. Many people prefer living in a small town to living in a big city. 2. There's friendliness in small towns, they say. 3. Crime is lower, and distances to and from work and school are shorter. 4. Many small-town mayors are Republicans.

A Sentence 1

B Sentence 2

C Sentence 3

D Sentence 4

4 1. Most people do not eat enough fruits and vegetables. 2. Turnips are round with a purple blush at one end. 3. Parsnips look a little like white carrots. 4. Rutabagas are light orange and have the most flavor of these root vegetables.

F Sentence 1

G Sentence 2

H Sentence 3

J Sentence 4

Check your answers on page 92.

Circle the letter of the answer that best develops the topic sentence.

1   Everyone should know how to change a car tire.

   A   You may find yourself in an emergency. Knowing how to change a flat tire might even save your life.

   B   Tires come in different sizes, depending on the vehicle. Off-road tires are usually bigger and have deeper treads.

   C   Everyone should also know how to start an emergency fire. Freezing to death is a real risk in some areas of the country.

   D   Some organizations offer emergency road help. However, you must usually become a member of the organization.

For numbers 2 and 3, read the paragraph. Then circle the letter of the sentence that best fills the blank in the paragraph.

2   _____. For some people, succeeding means earning a lot of money. For others, it means having good friends. For still others, it means doing the best you can with what you have.

   F   Why is success so hard to find?

   G   It's good to have money and friends.

   H   People judge success in different ways.

   J   The most successful people are those who can focus well.

3   Jan tried to turn into the hardware store parking lot. _____ Fire trucks were spraying water on the blazing building. Police were directing traffic away from the lot.

   A   She flipped on her turn signal.

   B   She needed a washer for the kitchen faucet.

   C   She decided to go to a different hardware store.

   D   She saw that the old hardware store was in flames!

Read the paragraph. Then circle the letter of the sentence that does not belong in the paragraph.

4   1. The first day at a new job can be a hectic experience for anyone. 2. There's so much information to take in, from new people to new responsibilities. 3. Employment agencies can be very helpful in finding people a new job. 4. However, with time, almost everyone begins to feel at home at a new workplace.

   F   Sentence 1

   G   Sentence 2

   H   Sentence 3

   J   Sentence 4

Check your answers on page 92.

Lesson 23 | Capitalization

Writers use capital letters in many situations. The most common situation is at the beginning of every sentence. However, there are many other situations in which you need to use capital letters. The TABE will ask you to choose words and sentences that are capitalized correctly.

Example **Read the paragraph. Notice all of the capitalized words.**

Tim and Sheila spent the day in New York City last Labor Day, which is the first Monday in September. They planned their day using the travel section of *The New York Times*. First they went to the Empire State Building, which is on Fifth Avenue. Then they went to the Metropolitan Museum of Art, where they saw an exhibit of Vincent Van Gogh's paintings. Sheila especially liked Van Gogh's "Starry Night." After an exciting day of sightseeing, Tim and Sheila went to see the musical play *Cats* and had dinner at the Broadway Deli.

This paragraph has many capitalized words. The first letter of every sentence is capitalized. There are several other kinds of capitalized words in this paragraph. Those words are shown in the table below.

Kind of Word	Examples
Personal names	Tim, Sheila, Vincent Van Gogh
Place names: streets, buildings, places, and locations	Empire State Building, Fifth Avenue, New York City, Metropolitan Museum of Art, Broadway Deli
Months	September
Days of the week	Monday
Holidays	Labor Day
Names of publications, works of art	*The New York Times*, "Starry Night," *Cats*

Test Example

Read the sentences. Then circle the letter of the sentence that uses capitalization correctly.

1 A   the train left on monday for Seattle.

   B   Does Charlie have to work on Presidents' day?

   C   Elizabeth read about the crash in *The Boston Globe*.

   D   Mr. Franklin spoke to the book Club at Elm Street school about the novel *Jaws*.

1 C *Elizabeth* and *The Boston Globe* are correctly capitalized. In option A, the first word and *Monday* are not capitalized. In option B, *Day*, part of the name of a holiday, should be capitalized. In option D, *club* should not be capitalized and *school* should be.

Practice

For numbers 1 to 3, circle the letter of the sentence that is written correctly.

1
A Thanksgiving is always the fourth Thursday in November.

B William and Robin are going to Myrtle Beach next Month.

C The TV Tower on Belmont Hill is the tallest building in the State.

D We went to the movie Theater and saw the new Bruce Willis Movie.

2
F Mr. Vasquez works at the Center City Café on third Street.

G The Chicago Cubs play at Wrigley Field each Summer.

H Would you like to come over for dinner next Tuesday?

J Her Daughter Jackie was born on the Fourth of July.

3
A The song "Hey Jude" by the beatles came on the radio.

B The boy's name on the show *Lassie* was Timmy.

C I have to take my car to Franklin Street Garage next Monday Morning.

D If you ever get a chance to read the Book *The Shining*, be sure to read it!

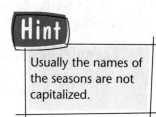

Hint

Usually the names of the seasons are not capitalized.

For numbers 4 to 6, read the paragraph and look at the numbered, underlined portions. Circle the letter of the answer that is written correctly for each underlined portion.

(4)   Lonnie saw an ad in the *Montgomery journal* that looked promising. He called up Montgomery Glassworks and asked
(5)   to speak to Ms. Antoinette Mitchell. she asked him to come in for
(6)   an interview a week from this Friday. Lonnie crossed his fingers.

4
F an Ad in the *Montgomery journal*

G an ad in the *Montgomery Journal*

H an ad in the *montgomery journal*

J Correct as it is

5
A to speak to ms. Antoinette Mitchell. She

B to speak to Ms. Antoinette mitchell. She

C to speak to Ms. Antoinette Mitchell. She

D Correct as it is

6
F a Week from this Friday. Lonnie

G a week from this Friday. lonnie

H a Week from this friday. Lonnie

J Correct as it is

Check your answers on pages 92–93.

Lesson 24 End Marks

A complete sentence always ends with a punctuation mark. The purpose of punctuation is to make writing clear and to communicate emotion and meaning. But when is it correct to use a period, question mark, or exclamation point? See if you know the rules for end punctuation. The TABE will ask you to choose which punctuation a sentence needs.

Example **Read these sentences. Write the correct end mark on the blank line at the end of each sentence.**

Sometimes our children seem to know just how to get us angry _____

Keep reading to find out what you can do about this problem _____

These sentences need periods. A sentence that makes a statement should end with a period. Most sentences that make commands should end with a period.

Example **Read the sentence. Write the correct end mark on the blank line at the end of the sentence.**

How does your child push your buttons _____

This sentence needs a question mark. A sentence that asks a question should end with a question mark.

Example **Read the sentence. Write in the correct end mark at the end of the sentence.**

That's not fair _____

This sentence needs an exclamation point. A sentence that shows strong feelings should end with an exclamation point. If you are unsure of when to use end marks before you take the TABE, study the chart below.

Period	Sentences that make statements or commands end with periods. *It is important to learn the rules of punctuation.*
Question mark	Sentences that ask a question end with question marks. *Now do you understand?*
Exclamation point	Sentences that show emotion, surprise, or strong feelings end with exclamation points. *You're really ready now!*

Test Example

Read the sentence and look at the underlined word and end mark. Choose the answer that uses the correct end mark.

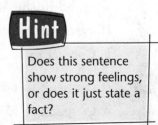

Hint

Does this sentence show strong feelings, or does it just state a fact?

1 Our children have learned ways to get us to react to <u>them.</u>

   A them!   **C** them

   B them?   **D** Correct as it is

1 D This statement should end with a period, so it is correct as it is. It does not express strong feelings that would require an exclamation point (option A). It is also not a question (option B). It is a complete sentence, so it must have an end mark (option C).

Practice

For numbers 1 and 2, decide which punctuation mark, if any, is needed in each sentence.

1 Your children are constantly trying to get your attention

A !

B ?

C .

D None

2 How should you deal with this situation

F !

G ?

H .

J None

For numbers 3 and 4, look at the underlined portions. Choose the answer that is written correctly for each underlined portion.

3 Your younger child screams, "He's touching me."

A me!"

B me?"

C me"

D Correct as it is

4 "No, I'm not!" the older one yells back!

F back.

G back?

H back!"

J Correct as it is

For Numbers 5 and 6, choose the sentence that shows the correct end mark.

5 A First do your best to stay out of it?

B Then give them your attention in a positive way.

C Show them this is not the way to get your attention

D Encourage them to work it out between themselves!

6 F Here are some responses that might sound familiar!

G Remember that this stage, too, will pass in time?

H What should you avoid saying!

J Parenting isn't easy!

Check your answers on page 93.

Commas are punctuation marks that divide parts of sentences. They are the most frequently used punctuation marks. This lesson explains and gives examples of some of the comma's uses. The TABE will ask you to select sentences that use commas correctly.

Examples **Read the sentences. Notice the commas in each sentence. The rules for each comma use follow the example.**

Example My favorite foods are chicken, beans, and rice.

When to Use Series Commas
- Use series commas when you have a list of three or more items grouped in a series.
- Use the series comma with groups of three that include more than one word.
    I like Mexican food, watching TV, and going to flea markets.

Example Henry and I went out to dinner in Chicago, Illinois.

When to Use City and State Commas
- Always place a comma between the city and state name.
- Use another comma after the state name if it is within a sentence.
    Henry and I went out to dinner in Chicago, Illinois, at the restaurant where we first met.

Example It's time to eat, Henry, so sit down at the table.

When to Use Direct Address Commas
- Always use a comma after a direct address. Direct address is when you speak directly to a person, using that person's name.
- A direct address can be at the beginning, middle, or end of a sentence.
- If the direct address comes at the beginning of a sentence, follow it with a comma.
    Henry, it's time to eat.
- If a direct address comes at the end of a sentence it should be preceded by a comma.
    It's time to eat, Henry.
- If the direct address comes in the middle of a sentence, it should be enclosed by commas.
    All I am saying, Henry, is use your napkin.

Example Henry and I were very hungry, but we could not finish our meal.

When to Use Compound Sentence Commas
- Use a comma to separate the two parts of a compound sentence.
- The comma precedes the coordinating conjunction (*and, but, yet, or, nor, for, because*).

Read the paragraph and look at the underlined portion. Circle the letter of the answer that is written correctly for the underlined portion.

1   Rosie <u>paid the attendant, drove into the parking garage and, parked the car.</u> When she got out of her car, she noticed that her taillight had been smashed.

   A   paid the attendant drove into the parking garage, and parked the car.

   B   paid the attendant, drove into the parking garage, and, parked the car.

   C   paid the attendant, drove into the parking garage, and parked the car.

   D   Correct as it is

1   C In option C, series commas follow *attendant* and *garage*. In option A, there should be a comma after *attendant*. In option B, there is an extra comma after *and*. In option D, there is a comma after *and* but not after *garage*.

Practice

For numbers 1 and 2, read the paragraph and look at the numbered, underlined portions. Circle the letter of the answer that is written correctly for each underlined portion.

(1)   Hey! <u>Take a look, at this jacket Al.</u> I found it on the rack over there. The
(2)   label says it's <u>from a store in, Atlanta Georgia.</u> Maybe I'll buy it. I think it's a real bargain at this price.

1   A Take a look at this jacket Al.

   B Take a look, at this jacket, Al.

   C Take a look at this jacket, Al.

   D Correct as it is

2   F from a store in Atlanta, Georgia,

   G from a store in Atlanta, Georgia.

   H from a store, in Atlanta Georgia.

   J Correct as it is

For numbers 3 and 4, choose which punctuation mark, if any, is needed in the sentence.

3   The test question was difficult but I figured out the answer.

   A ,

   B .

   C ?

   D None

4   Barbara closed her eyes, held her breath and pushed the button to release the parachute.

   F ,

   G .

   H !

   J None

Check your answers on page 93.

For numbers 1 and 2, choose which punctuation mark, if any, is needed in the sentence.

1   Reggie your son is on the phone.

   A ,   **B** !   **C** ?   **D** None

2   Do you want me to tell him you'll call him back, or shall I ask him to hold

   F .   **G** ,   **H** ?   **J** None

For numbers 3 and 4, read the paragraph and look at the numbered, underlined portions. Circle the letter of the answer that is written correctly for each underlined portion.

(3)   Power tools such as saws, lathes, planers and drills definitely

(4)   make a job easier and faster. But you have to be careful. last october, my Brother-in-Law Burt almost cut off his thumb.

3   **A** Power tools such as saws, lathes, planers, and, drills

   B Power tools such as saws, lathes, planers, and drills

   C Power tools such as saws, lathes, planers and, drills

   D Correct as it is

4   **F** last October, my brother-in-law Burt

   G Last october, my Brother-in-Law burt

   H Last October, my brother-in-law Burt

   J Correct as it is

For number 5, circle the letter of the sentence that is written correctly.

5   **A** The famous Highway starts in Chicago, Illinois.

   B It passes through Gallup, New Mexico, and Kingman, Arizona.

   C have you heard the song about the route?

   D Nat King cole really knows how to sing!

For number 6, choose the sentence that shows the correct end mark.

6   **F** Who are some of your sister's very favorite singers.

   G She likes to hear harmony and beautiful melodies!

   H I can't believe some of the stuff kids listen to today?

   J Soul music from the 1960s is my favorite.

Check your answers on page 93.

Lesson 26 Quotation Marks

Quotation marks enclose quotations, which are the exact words that people speak. They indicate something that has been said. The box below lists rules for using quotation marks.

Rules for Using Quotation Marks

• When the direct quotation is a complete sentence, it begins with a capital letter.
    Mario said, "**T**he game starts at eight o'clock."
• When the quote is a sentence fragment, it does not begin with a capital letter.
    Mario said the basketball game was "**t**he best ever."
• Use a comma after phrases such as *Mario said* when they come before the quotation.
    Mario said**,** "Give me the basketball."
• Use a comma, followed by quotation marks, after the last word of a quotation when it is followed by a phrase, such as *Mario said*.
    "It's time to leave for practice**,"** Mario said.
• Question marks and exclamation points are placed <u>inside</u> the quotation mark when they are part of the quotation.
    The umpire asked, "Are the players ready**?"**
• Question marks and exclamation points are placed <u>outside</u> the quotation mark when they are <u>not</u> part of the quotation.
    Were you surprised when I said, "I'd love to come to the game"**?**

Example **Read the sentences. Which sentence includes a direct quotation?**_____

> **Sentence 1** Mario said, "I'm taking my ball and going home!"
> **Sentence 2** Mario said he would take his ball and go home.

Sentence 1 is a direct quotation, so it includes quotation marks. The second sentence is *not* a direct quotation. It does not repeat the exact words Mario said.

Test Example

Read the sentences. Then circle the letter of the sentence that is written correctly.

1 A It's too hot to play basketball Jimmie groaned.

 B Andrew asked? "What's the temperature, anyway."

 C "It's too bad," added Mario, "there aren't any trees around the court."

 D "I'd plant one," Jimmie answered "with another groan, but it's too hot."

1 **C** In option A, there should be quotation marks around Jimmie's words and the comma following the quotation. In option B, the question mark is placed incorrectly after *asked*. It should follow *anyway*. There should also be a comma after *asked*. In option D, *with another groan* are not Jimmie's words, so the quotation marks should be placed right before *but*.

Practice

For numbers 1 and 2, choose the punctuation mark, if any, that is needed in the sentence.

1 The butler stood in the doorway and announced, Dinner is served."

A   ,

B   "

C   .

D   None

2 Suddenly the lights went out, and someone shouted, "There's a hand on my arm!"

F   "

G   ,

H   .

J   None

For numbers 3 and 4, circle the letter of the sentence that is written correctly.

3

A   Was that a shot? someone asked in a frightened voice.

B   "Someone please turn on the lights," a woman's voice said.

C   Mr. Dain-Hutton said, I think I heard someone running out the door."

D   "Please look behind the sofa" added Mrs. Stoycheff. "because I heard a moan."

4

F   Major Wennington lit a match and said "Perhaps this match will help".

G   "A gasp" went around the room when they saw what had happened.

H   Major Wennington called out, "Sir Andrew has been murdered!"

J   "Oh, cried Sir Andrew's wife, I think I am going to faint."

For numbers 5 and 6, read the paragraph and look at the numbered, underlined portions. Circle the letter of the answer that is written correctly for each underlined portion.

(5)   "Please remain calm, <u>ladies and gentlemen" the little detective</u> said. "I'm afraid no one will be permitted to leave the house.

(6)   There's been a terrible murder committed <u>here," he added. "and,</u> <u>with your help,</u> I intend to solve this crime."

5

A   ladies and gentlemen, the little detective said."

B   ladies and gentlemen." the little detective said.

C   ladies and gentlemen," the little detective said.

D   Correct as it is

6

F   here," he added, "and, with your help,

G   here." he added and, with your help,

H   here, he added. "and, with your help,

J   Correct as it is

Check your answers on pages 93–94.

Lesson 27 Apostrophe

Apostrophes are used in two important ways. They are used in contractions. A contraction is two words combined into one. All contractions include an apostrophe in the place where a letter or letters have been omitted. Apostrophes are also used to show ownership by making nouns possessive.

Example **Read the sentence. It includes a contraction with an apostrophe. What**

letter has been dropped out of the contraction? _____

It's not easy living next door to a kennel.

The letter that the apostrophe is replacing is the *i* in *is*. *It's* is a contraction of the words "it is."

Example **Read the sentence. It includes an apostrophe. What does the apostrophe**

say about the toy? _____

That is the dog's toy.

The apostrophe says that the toy belongs to the dog. It shows the dog's ownership of the toy. When forming possessives, be sure not to confuse *'s* with just *s*.
- *Dog's* means "belonging to the dog."
- *Dogs* means "more than one dog," as in "*It sounds as though there are eight barking dogs outside.*"

Test Example

Read the sentences. Circle the letter of the sentence that is written correctly.

1   A   Its very hard to get any sleep with that dog barking all night.

    B   I will call the police if they don't do something about the barking.

    C   That dogs bark is so loud we cannot hear our stereo or television.

    D   My other neighbors dog is very well trained and does not bark at all.

Many people confuse *its* and *it's*. *Its* is a possessive pronoun and *it's* is a contraction of *it is*.

1 B This sentence includes an apostrophe in *don't* ("do not"). In option A , the apostrophe in *It's* ("It is") is omitted. In option C, the apostrophe in *dog's* is missing. In option D, the apostrophe that belongs in *neighbor's* is omitted.

Practice

For numbers 1 through 3, read the paragraph and look at the numbered, underlined portions. Circle the letter of the answer that is written correctly for each underlined portion.

(1) <u>Daniels friends</u> at work decided to throw a surprise birthday
(2) party for him. He was turning 40. <u>His friends were afraid hed find out</u>, so they were very careful. The party was planned for
(3) Saturday night for a nearby restaurant. <u>The restaurants manager was a friend of one of the planners.</u>

1 A Daniel's friends
   B Daniels' friends
   C Daniel's friend's
   D Correct as it is

2 F His friend's were afraid he'd find out,
   G His friends were afraid he'd find out,
   H His friends were afraid h'ed find out,
   J Correct as it is

3 A The restaurant's manager was a friend of one of the planner's.
   B The restaurants' manager was a friend of one of the planners.
   C The restaurant's manager was a friend of one of the planners.
   D Correct as it is

For numbers 4 through 6, circle the letter of the sentence that is written correctly.

4 F That cars headlights are shining in my eyes.
   G Id get those headlights fixed if that were my car.
   H This stores parking lot must be the biggest in town.
   J I am going inside to buy a present for my daughter's birthday.

5 A I'm not sure what is wrong with the car.
   B Your'e not planning to drive that car to the party, are you?
   C We can borrow one of my moms cars to go to church on Sunday.
   D The brakes did not seem to work when I stopped at my friends house.

6 F What is Rudys telephone number?
   G I think its' written on the refrigerator.
   H Call him to tell him we'll be late picking him up.
   J I have not met his new girlfriend, but I hear shes nice.

Check your answers on page 94.

Knowing the proper format for writing letters can help you apply for jobs and schools and write business and personal correspondence. It is important that your letters are written correctly. The TABE will ask you to choose correctly written parts of a letter.

Example **Review the following parts of a letter.**

December 3, 2003

Looksharp Hat Company
786 Washington Boulevard
Mount Vernon, Ohio 43050

Dear Director of Sales:

The body of the letter goes here. It communicates your message. Effective letters are succinct and professional.

Sincerely,

Campbell Phillips

Campbell Phillips

Letters always begin with the date in the upper right-hand corner. The month is capitalized, and the day is followed by a comma.

The inside address appears in the left margin, a line or two below the date. It is the address to which you are sending the letter. It follows standard capitalization rules. A comma follows the city name, but not the state name.

The salutation includes the name or position of the person you're sending the letter to. The name or position follows *Dear* and ends with a colon. When sending a letter addressed to a position or a department, always capitalize each word of the position, except prepositions like *of*.

In the body of the letter, write your message, following all rules of grammar, capitalization, and punctuation.

Close your letter with a phrase like *Sincerely, Yours truly,* or *Respectfully yours,* followed by a comma. Then sign and type your full name.

Test Example

Look at the underlined word of this business letter. Circle the letter of the answer that is written correctly for the underlined portion.

1   I look forward to hearing from you in the next week.

<u>sincerely,</u>

Rachel McDonald

Rachel McDonald

A   Sincerely.

B   Sincerely

C   Sincerely,

D   Correct as it is

1 C Option C begins with a capital letter and is followed by a comma. Option A is followed by a period where there should be a comma. Option B has no punctuation. Option D does not begin with a capital letter.

Practice

Read the letter and look at the numbered, underlined portions. Circle the letter of the answer that is written correctly for each underlined portion.

(1) april 12, 2003

Jollyland Theme Park
(2) p.o. Box 808
(3) 5670 West Newcastle road
(4) Richmond, Indiana, 47374

(5) Dear Personnel Manager:

I am writing in response to the ad you placed in the *Daily News* for clowns to work at Jollyland this summer. I am an experienced clown. I am including a list of references and a resume of my experiences in clowning, theater, and working with children. Thank you for considering me for a clown position at your theme park. I look forward to hearing from you.

(6) yours truly,

James Ling

James Ling

1
A April 12 2003
B April 12, 2003
C April, 12 2003
D Correct as it is

2
F P.O. Box 808
G p.o. box 808
H P.O. box 808
J Correct as it is

3
A 5670, West Newcastle Road
B 5670 West newcastle road
C 5670 West Newcastle Road
D Correct as it is

4
F Richmond, indiana 47374
G Richmond, Indiana 47374
H richmond, Indiana 47374
J Correct as it is

5
A Dear Personnel Manager
B dear Personnel Manager:
C Dear personnel Manager:
D Correct as it is

6
F Yours Truly,
G Yours Truly
H Yours truly,
J Correct as it is

Check your answers on page 94.

Circle the letter of the punctuation mark, if any, that is needed in the sentence.

1   "Do you know what a glacier is" Mark asked.

    A ?   **B** "   **C** .   **D** None

For numbers 2 and 3, circle the letter of the sentence that is written correctly.

2
  F   Sandie has happy memories of her familys' camping vacations.

  G   "I can still remember how early we used to get up, she said."

  H   She's not sure if she could go camping with her own family.

  J   Sandie hadnt mentioned anything about going fishing.

3
  A   Sandie said. "This sleeping bag is really uncomfortable."

  B   Vern, Sandies husband, does not really like camping.

  C   Get away from that fire!" Vern screamed.

  D   They probably won't go camping again.

Read the letter and look at the numbered, underlined portions. Circle the letter of the answer that is written correctly for each underlined portion.

>   **(4)** November, 15 2003
>
>   Prospect Manufacturing Company
> **(5)** 512 Main Street
> **(6)** Wakefield Rhode Island, 02879
>
>   Dear Sales Manager:
>
>   I am returning this flashlight, which I bought at a local store. The spring that holds the batteries in place broke after five minutes of use. I would like you to replace the flashlight or refund my money. Thank you for taking care of this matter.
>
>   Sincerely,
>   *Rebecca Johnston*
>   Rebecca Johnston

4
  F   November 15 2003

  G   november 15, 2003

  H   November 15, 2003

  J   Correct as it is

5
  A   512 main street

  B   512 Main street

  C   512 main Street

  D   Correct as it is

6
  F   Wakefield, rhode Island 02879

  G   Wakefield, Rhode Island 02879

  H   Wakefield, Rhode Island, 02879

  J   Correct as it is

Check your answers on pages 94–95.

Lesson 29 Vowels

Vowels are the letters *a, e, i, o, u*, and sometimes *y*. Here are the four different types of vowel sounds that are on the TABE.

Vowels
Short Vowels
• Most small words with one vowel in the middle have a short vowel sound.
• Some short vowels are spelled with a combination of letters.   An example is the **ea** in heavy.
• A short vowel sound <u>cannot</u> come at the end a word.
Long Vowels
• In general, long vowels are pronounced like the name of the letter.   For example, the **a** in *newspaper* is pronounced like the name of the letter **a**.
• Some long vowel sounds are spelled with a combination of letters.   Examples are the **ai** in *daily* and the **ea** in *season*.
Schwa
• This vowel sound sounds like "uh" and is often spelled with an **a**, but can also be spelled with an **e**, **i**, or **o**.   Examples of the schwa sound include temper**a**ture and am**a**teur.
R-Controlled Vowel
• When the letter **r** follows a vowel, the vowel usually changes its sound.   For example, compare *bat* and *bar*, *fat* and *far*, or *sit* and *sir*.

Example **Say the sentence aloud and think about how the highlighted vowels sound. They're examples of *short* vowels.**

The l**a**st not**i**ce s**a**id s**o**mething about n**o**t l**i**fting h**ea**vy **o**bj**e**cts.

Test Example

Read the sentence. Circle the letter of the word that is spelled correctly and that best completes the sentence.

1 Can you _____ the prices in this store?

   A beleave   C believe

   B beleive   D beleve

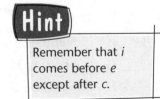

Hint

Remember that *i* comes before *e* except after *c*.

> 1 **C** When you are spelling the long *e* vowel sound, the letter combination *ie* is more common than *ei*. Options A, B, and D are all misspelled.

Lesson 30 | Consonants

Consonants are all the letters except the vowels *a, e, i, o,* and *u.* The letter *y* can be either a vowel *or* a consonant. Different consonant sounds can be spelled in different ways.

Example **Speak the sentence aloud and think about how the highlighted consonants sound. What do they have in common?** _____

Maria lost the re**c**ipe in the vi**c**inity of the gro**c**ery store.

They all represent the consonant sound *s* spelled with *c.* Many words are spelled with one consonant, but pronounced with the sound of a different consonant. This is called a **variant spelling**. Here is another example.

The sol**d**iers marched around the track. The *d* in *soldiers* sounds like a *j.*

Example **Speak the sentence aloud and think about how the highlighted consonants sound. What do the *n* in *solemn* and the *c* in *descend* have in common?** _____

The crowd watched with solem**n** faces as the plane des**c**ended from the sky.

The *n* in *solemn* and the *c* in *descend* are not pronounced. This is called a **silent letter**. To correctly spell words with silent consonants, you have to include these letters.

Example **Read the sentence aloud. In this example, the highlighted consonants are doubled. Doubling a consonant does not change the ways it's pronounced.**

Fran's a**pp**etite returned, and she reached acro**ss** the table for the potatoes.

Some other examples of words with double consonants are *possession, cancellation,* and *attract.*

Test Example

Circle the letter of the word that is spelled correctly and best completes the sentence.

1 The accident victim seemed to be _____.

    A concious   **C** conshus

    B consious   **D** conscious

> The letter *c* sounds like *s* when followed by *i* or *e.* It sounds like *k* when followed by *a, o,* or *u.*

1 **D** Even though the consonant sound is a *sh* sound, the word is spelled with the letter combination *sci.* Options A, B, and C are misspelled.

The TABE will test your spelling on other kinds of words and letter combinations. This lesson will help you learn more about these kinds of TABE questions.

Examples **Read the sentences. Answer the questions.**

What do the two underlined words have in common?

Homonym

Did Bill write down the right message?

Write and *right* are pronounced exactly the same. However, they are two completely different words with different meanings. This kind of word is called a **homonym**.

Read the sentence. Notice the underlined words. What observation can you make about the word *beginning*? _____

Root   Suffix

With any task, it's best to begin at the beginning.

Beginning is based on the word *begin.* A word on which other words is based is called a **root**. The ending is called a **suffix**.

Read the sentence. Write the correct letter or letters on the blank line to complete the underlined word.

The stew had beef, onions, carrots, beans, and lots of potato_____ in it.

Did you write –es on the line? Some words that end in *o* add an *e* before the *s* when they become plural.

Read the sentence. Write the correct letter or letters in the blank to complete the underlined word.

Hailstorms are not very frequ_____ around here.

Did you write in -ent? Endings like *-ance*, *-ence*, *-ant*, and *-ent* are easy to confuse, because there's no clear clue to the spelling. Memorizing words helps. You can also get spelling clues from similar words. For example, *frequent* is similar to *frequency.* You can make an educated guess that *frequent* is also spelled with an *e* in the last syllable like *frequency.*

Test Example

Circle the letter of the word that is spelled correctly and best completes the sentence.

1 That's the most _____ beach I have ever seen.

   A beautiful   **C** beutiful

   B beautifull   **D** beautyful

1 **A** In option A, the suffix or ending *-ful* is added to the root *beauty* to form *beautiful.* The *y* in beauty changes to an *i* when the suffix is added. Options B, C, and D are misspelled.

Circle the letter of the word that is spelled correctly and best completes the sentence.

1 The weather report called for _____ rain showers tomorrow.

A frequant

B frequont

C frequint

D frequent

2 Frank, the stereo is no longer in my _____.

F possession

G posesion

H possesion

J posession

3 Cicely asked that her records be _____ to another hospital.

A transferrd

B transfered

C transferred

D transferd

4 The lake _____ in northern Michigan was breathtaking!

F seenery

G senery

H scenery

J scenry

5 Do you feel that your health insurance is _____?

A adaquate

B adequate

C adequat

D adequit

6 Adam is one of the most _____ people I know.

F sinsere

G sinceer

H sincere

J sincire

7 You bring me so much _____.

A happyness

B happiness

C happieness

D hapiness

8 The whole country followed the progress of the _____.

F soljers

G solgers

H soldiers

J soldeirs

9 What's your favorite _____ of the year?

A season

B seeson

C seison

D seson

10 The whale at the aquarium was
_____!

F enormus

G enormuos

H enormuss

J enormous

11 Brad _____ he had made a good
decision.

A new

B neu

C knew

D knue

12 Knowing how to use a computer is a big
_____ to someone looking for a job.

F advantage

G advanige

H advanage

J advantige

13 It seems as though the presidential
election _____ goes on forever!

A campain

B campane

C campaine

D campaign

14 Becky stayed home from work because
her son had a high _____.

F temperture

G temperature

H tempirature

J tempurature

15 Twanda had a big _____ after
hiking.

A apitite

B appitite

C apetite

D appetite

16 This is my favorite _____ for
carrots.

F recippe

G resippe

H recipe

J resipe

17 I always _____ when I ride the
roller coaster.

A scream

B screem

C screme

D screame

18 Truthfulness is an important _____
in relationships.

F qualety

G quality

H quallity

J quallety

19 Can you pick up one _____ donuts?

A dosen

B dusen

C duzen

D dozen

Check your answers on page 95.

The Language Performance Assessment is identical to the real TABE in format and length. It will give you an idea of what the real test is like. Allow yourself 39 minutes to complete this assessment. Check your answers on pages 95–98.

Sample A

A Dan and I are cooking dinner for our friends.

B Reaching for the jar on the top shelf.

C Tim ate at a restaurant tomorrow.

D I gave they the cookbook.

Sample B

F I think I'll cut the grass

G Is it supposed to rain on saturday?

H Do you think the lawn mower will start.

J I just changed the spark plug on the mower.

Sample C

The girls picked out a bag of apples.

The apples were juicy.

A The girls picked out a bag of apples, and they were juicy.

B The girls picked out and juiced a bag of apples.

C The girls picked out a bag of juicy apples.

D The girls picked out a bag of apples that were juicy.

Sample D

Has Ellen bought her tickets yet. we bought ours last week.

F yet. We

G yet, we

H yet? We

J Correct as it is

For numbers 1 through 3, circle the letter of the word or phrase that best completes the sentence.

1   The party guests arrived _____ than Marsha expected.

    A   more soonly

    B   more sooner

    C   soonest

    D   sooner

2   That dog _____ more food than any other dog I know.

    F   have eaten

    G   are eating

    H   eats

    J   eat

3   Have your children ever _____ to summer camp?

    A   going

    B   gone

    C   went

    D   go

For numbers 4 through 8, read the underlined sentences. Then circle the letter of the sentence that best combines those sentences into one.

4   Herb wanted to make tacos for dinner.

The grocery store was out of taco shells.

    F   The grocery store was out of taco shells because Herb wanted to make tacos for dinner.

    G   Herb wanted to make tacos for dinner at the grocery store, but he was out of taco shells.

    H   Herb wanted to make tacos for dinner, but the grocery store was out of taco shells.

    J   Herb wanted to make tacos for dinner, but he was out of taco shells.

5   Jill bought a new DVD player.

She bought the DVD player at the mall.

    A   Jill bought a new DVD player at the mall.

    B   Jill bought a DVD player at the new mall.

    C   The DVD player at the mall is new that Jill bought.

    D   Jill bought a new DVD player, and she bought the DVD player at the mall.

6 The washing machine is in the basement.

The dryer is in the basement.

F The washing machine is in the basement, and the dryer is in the basement.

G The washing machine is and the dryer is in the basement, too.

H The washing machine, the dryer are in the basement.

J The washing machine and dryer are in the basement.

7 Sandie went to the football game last night.

Rose and Thomas went to the football game last night.

A Sandie, Rose, and Thomas went to the football game last night.

B Sandie went to the football game last night, then Rose and Thomas went to the football game.

C Sandie went to the football game last night, and Rose and Thomas went to the football game, too.

D Sandie went to the football game last night, and Rose and Thomas went to the football game last night.

8 Charlie completed the test in 45 minutes.

He completed it quickly.

He completed it easily.

F Charlie completed the test, and he completed it quickly and easily in 45 minutes.

G In 45 quick and easy minutes, Charlie completed the test.

H Charlie quickly and easily completed the test in 45 minutes.

J Charlie completed the quick and easy test in 45 minutes.

For numbers 9 and 10, circle the letter of the sentence that does not belong in the paragraph.

9 1. The right to vote is a very important one. 2. However, as many as half of all eligible Americans do not bother to vote. 3. Most people vote on special machines. 4. Experts wonder what can be done to improve voting participation.

A Sentence 1

B Sentence 2

C Sentence 3

D Sentence 4

10 1. Many immigrants who came to the United States landed at Ellis Island in New York Harbor. 2. The Statue of Liberty was a gift from France. 3. It has stood in New York Harbor since 1886. 4. The famous statue is a symbol of freedom to people all over the world.

F Sentence 1

G Sentence 2

H Sentence 3

J Sentence 4

For numbers 11 through 14, read the paragraph and look at the numbered, underlined portions. Circle the letter of the answer that is written correctly for each underlined portion.

(11)   I visited two of our <u>newer</u> national parks this year. They show the great

(12) contrasts in the U.S. park system. <u>Denali National Park in alaska</u> contains the

(13) highest mountain in the United States. During my visit, I <u>will gaze</u> in wonder

at the mighty mountain. Death Valley National Park in California is the

lowest point in the entire Western Hemisphere. Both parks offer many

(14) beautiful views to people who visit <u>her</u>.

11   A newy

B more new

C more newer

D Correct as it is

13   A am gazing

B gazed

C are gazing

D Correct as it is

12   F denali National Park in Alaska

G Denali National Park in Alaska

H Denali National Park In Alaska

J Correct as it is

14   F it

G him

H them

J Correct as it is

For numbers 15 through 21, read the paragraph and look at the numbered, underlined portions. Circle the letter of the answer that is written correctly for each underlined portion.

(15)   <u>June, 16 2003</u>

South Oregon Medical Clinic

(16)   <u>51 High Street</u>

(17)   <u>Ashland, oregon 97520</u>

(18)   <u>Dear Dr Edwards:</u>

I will be moving to Seattle next month to take a

(19) new job at the <u>*Seattle weekly*</u>. Would you please prepare

(20) a copy of <u>my</u> medical records to take with me? I

(21) <u>will picking</u> them up at your office next week. I would

also be interested to know if you can recommend a

family doctor in the Seattle area. Thank you very much.

Sincerely,

Steve Hodges

Steve Hodges

15
  A June 16, 2003
  B june 16, 2003
  C June 16 2003
  D Correct as it is

16
  F 51 high Street
  G 51 High street
  H 51 High, Street
  J Correct as it is

17
  A Ashland, Oregon, 97520
  B Ashland, Oregon 97520
  C ashland, Oregon 97520
  D Correct as it is

18
  F Dear Dr. Edwards:
  G dear dr. Edwards:
  H Dear Dr. Edwards;
  J Correct as it is

19
  A *seattle Weekly*
  B *Seattle Weekly*
  C *seattle weekly*
  D Correct as it is

20
  F me
  G I's
  H my's
  J Correct as it is

21
  A picked
  B have picked
  C will pick
  D Correct as it is

For numbers 22 through 25, read the paragraph and look at the numbered, underlined portions. Circle the letter of the answer that is written correctly for each underlined portion.

(22)   The United States has always attracted immigrants from other <u>countries. in</u>

(23) 1960 the four leading homelands of immigrants were <u>Italy, Germany, Canada,</u>

<u>and Great Britain.</u> Since 1960, the percentage of immigrants from developing

(24) countries has increased <u>great.</u> More than a quarter of all immigrants now

(25) come from Mexico. Next in number are <u>the philippines, China, and Vietnam.</u>

22 **F** countries. In
    G countries, In
    H countries in
    J Correct as it is

24 **F** more great
    G greater
    H greatly
    J Correct as it is

23 **A** Italy Germany, Canada, and Great Britain
    B Italy, Germany, Canada, and Great, Britain
    C Italy, Germany, Canada and, Great Britain
    D Correct as it is

25 **A** the Philippines, China, And Vietnam
    B the Philippines, China, and Vietnam
    C the philippines, china, and vietnam
    D Correct as it is

For numbers 26 through 30, read the paragraph and look at the numbered, underlined portions. Circle the letter of the answer that is written correctly for each underlined portion.

(26)   Do you enjoy <u>working in your yard or get together with your friends</u> on summer

evenings? If you do, you are probably grateful for Daylight Savings Time. It's an

(27) idea <u>what</u> many people take advantage of. Daylight Savings Time means moving

the clock ahead one hour during the warmer months of the year. Daylight Savings

(28) Time <u>was</u> first adopted during World War I. Today, most states adopt D.S.T. to give

(29) <u>they</u> citizens a chance to spend more time outdoors. Three that do not use D.S.T.

(30) are <u>Arizona, Hawaii, and the eastern part of Indiana.</u>

26 **F** working in your yard or with your friends
    G to work in your yard or getting together with your friends
    H working in your yard or getting together with your friends
    J Correct as it is

27 **A** who
    B that
    C whom
    D Correct as it is

28
   F were
   G are
   H were being
   J Correct as it is

29
   A its
   B them
   C their
   D Correct as it is

30
   F Arizona, Hawaii and the eastern part of Indiana
   G Arizona, Hawaii, and the eastern part, of Indiana
   H Arizona, Hawaii and, the eastern part of Indiana
   J Correct as it is

For numbers 31 and 32, circle the letter of the answer that best develops the topic sentence.

31   Health care is one of the fastest-growing job categories.

   A As Americans grow older, more health care workers will be needed. These workers will find jobs in hospitals, clinics, and as home health-care aides.

   B Some people avoid going to the doctor, even when they are ill. This can make dealing with their medical problems more difficult.

   C Many Americans are overweight. More and more health care workers will be needed to help solve their medical problems.

   D Unemployment was quite low during the 1990s. In the past few years, however, the unemployment rate has increased.

32   The U.S. military has five branches.

   F Two of the best known are the Army and the Navy. The Army generally fights on land, while the Navy's focus is the world's oceans.

   G They are the Army, Navy, Air Force, Marines, and Coast Guard. Each has its own special duties, equipment, and leadership.

   H Former members of the military are called veterans. We honor them on November 11, Veterans' Day.

   J The largest is the Army. Close behind is the Navy, followed by the Air Force.

For numbers 33 through 37, circle the letter of the punctuation mark, if any, that is needed in the sentence.

33 If you look harder, Patty I'm sure you'll find your car keys.

    A "   **B** !   **C** ,   **D** None

34 "Do you think," Dave asked "that maybe you've seen this movie before?"

    F ,   **G** ?   **H** "   **J** None

35 Alexa answered the essay question and moved on to the next page.

    A !   **B** ?   **C** ,   **D** None

36 Football, basketball baseball, and car racing are my favorite sports to watch.

    F "   **G** ?   **H** ,   **J** None

37 Stop that

    A ,   **B** !   **C** "   **D** None

For numbers 38 through 41, read the sentences. Then circle the letter of the sentence that best fills the blank in the paragraph.

38 _____. I really enjoy warm weather and being near the ocean. Plus, my life is stressful, so I like just relaxing and doing nothing.

    F Everybody needs a vacation.

    G Have you ever been to Florida?

    H Packaged trips have gotten a lot cheaper.

    J Beach vacations are my favorite kind of vacation.

39 Sam let his dog Sadie out the back door. _____ Sadie sat barking at the frightened cat, which had climbed a tree.

    A She immediately began chasing after a cat.

    B The dog had been whining to go out.

    C He pushed open the screen door.

    D The dog loved to chase cats.

40 Artie waited for his son Jason outside the barbershop. Jason had been in the shop for over an hour. Then finally the door to the barbershop opened and Jason walked out. _____

    F Artie sat down on a bench to wait for Jason.

    G Jason gave the barber some money and put on his jacket.

    H Artie was shocked when he saw his son's green hair!

    J "March right back in there and have that dye taken out!" Artie ordered.

41 _____. First put some oil in a pan and turn on the stove. Pour in the popcorn, cover with a lid, and give the pan a shake. Keep shaking the pan so the popcorn doesn't burn as it pops.

    A Popcorn is a fairly healthy snack.

    B Making popcorn on the stove is easy.

    C Popcorn now comes in different colors and flavors.

    D It's the water in popcorn that heats up and makes the corn pop.

For numbers 42 through 55, circle the letter of the sentence that is written correctly and shows the correct capitalization and punctuation. Be sure the sentence you choose is complete.

42   **F** Isnt' that your brother in the Fourth of July parade?

    G I believe our town's parade is one of the largest in the state.

    H Whats the name of that cowboy riding the horse in the parade?

    J Even though it rained during last years parade, everyone had a great time.

43   **A** Anthony decided to take guitar lessons

    B Is he more interested in jazz or rock music.

    C Do you think he's too old to learn to play an instrument?

    D You're never too old to learn to do something that you've always wanted to do?

44   **F** Jared and I went to the movies we saw the new Bruce Willis film.

    G Jared didn't want to go I talked him into going.

    H Waiting in line forever to buy popcorn.

    J Neither one of us liked the movie.

45   **A** "I'm so happy we won." said a fan at the game.

    B The announcer asked? "How many people expected this"

    C "We played a pretty good game," the winning coach explained.

    D "Our schedule gets a whole lot tougher after this game, he added."

46
  F By the time they arrived, it has started to rain very hard.

  G They have planned for many months before they left on their trip.

  H The weather report have predicted sunshine for the weekend.

  J They had hoped to go to the zoo and the memorial.

47
  A This restaurant serves the best mexican food.

  B Nancy and her Daughter are working there as waitresses.

  C I heard your brother-in-law alan was looking for a new job.

  D Maybe Nancy could talk to the manager about hiring him as a cook.

48
  F The people who wanted to visit the construction site rised their hands.

  G A big crane rose the air conditioner to the top of the building.

  H The workers raised the flag above the construction site.

  J Do you raise early to get to your job on time?

49
  A The first concert on the tour was in Atlanta Georgia.

  B Then the band played two concerts in Orlando, Florida.

  C After taking a week off, the band flew to St. Louis: Missouri.

  D The tour ended with a weeklong concert series in Los Angeles; California.

50
  F Looking forward to the fishing trip.

  G Everyone helping with the planning.

  H We are getting up at 4:30 to get an early start on the trip.

  J Daryl, Tom, and Skip in one boat and Dave, Bill, and J.R. in another.

51
  A Have you found a new apartment yet.

  B I'm going to look at some tomorrow afternoon

  C I'm supposed to meet the landlord here at 12:45

  D In my opinion, this apartment is absolutely fantastic!

52
  F You shouldv'e called to say you were going to be late for dinner.

  G Are'nt there any telephones at the plant?

  H Its' rude not to let us know your plans.

  J We'll just begin without you.

53
  A What did you do on Valentine's Day?

  B The card shop on Main street was very busy.

  C Flower shops do a lot of business on the Holiday.

  D Next month the card shop will be busy for st. patrick's day.

54
  F Mr. Chang took his car to the car wash because they were very dirty.

  G He dropped his keys under the seat but found it right away.

  H Mr. Chang and his sisters take care of her mother.

  J His car is eight years old, but it still runs well.

55
  A When the Red Sox won the championship.

  B Breaking the hearts of their fans ever since.

  C They beat the Chicago Cubs in the World Series.

  D It was 1918 Babe Ruth was a member of the team.

STOP

Lesson 1 Practice (page 9)

1. **A** This pronoun takes the place of *William Cody* and is the subject of the sentence. Thus, the singular nominative pronoun *he* is correct. Option B refers to a female. Option C is plural. Option D is incorrect, as *him* is an objective pronoun.

2. **G** This pronoun also refers to *William Cody*, but it is the object of the verb *called*. The singular objective pronoun *him* should be used. Option F does not refer to a male. Option H is plural. Option J is incorrect, as *her* refers to a female.

3. **B** The singular objective pronoun *him* is the object of the preposition *about*. *Him* takes the place of *William Cody*. Option A is a nominative pronoun and also refers to a female. Option C is plural. Option D is incorrect, as *he* is a nominative pronoun.

4. **J** *It* is the subject of this sentence and a nominative pronoun. *It* refers to Buffalo Bill's show. Options F and G are plural and *show* is singular. Option H is male and *show* is neutral.

5. **D** The plural objective pronoun *them* refers to *people*. *Them* is the object of the preposition *of*. Options A and B are singular. Option C is a nominative pronoun.

6. **F** The singular objective pronoun *it* takes the place of *show*. *It* is the object of *enjoyed*. Option G is a nominative pronoun. Option H refers to a male. Option J is plural.

Lesson 2 Practice (page 11)

1. **C** *Which* is a relative pronoun that refers to *fair* and connects the two parts of the sentence. *It* (option A) is a pronoun that can only be used to take the place of the subject of a sentence. *Who* (option B) is a relative pronoun that refers to a person, not a thing. *When* (option D) is not a pronoun.

2. **F** *Their* is a plural possessive pronoun that refers to *people*. *Them* (option G) is an objective pronoun that can not show possession. *There* (option H) is an adverb, not a pronoun. *They're* (option J) is not a pronoun. It is a contraction of the words *they are*.

3. **D** *Whose* is a relative possessive pronoun that refers to *winner* and connects the two parts of the sentence. *His* (option A) and *Him* (option B) cannot connect parts of sentences. *Who's* (option C) is not a pronoun. It is a contraction of the words *who is*.

4. **H** *His* is a possessive pronoun that is singular and male and refers to *he*. *Him* (option F) cannot show possession. *There* (option G) is an adverb, not a pronoun. *Their* (option J) refers to more than one person.

5. **B** *Who* is a relative pronoun that refers to a person (*winner*) and connects the two parts of the sentence. Options A, C, and D (*what, which,* and *that*) are

relative pronouns that refer to a things, rather than persons.

6. **F** *Their* is a possessive pronoun used to refer to more than one person (*he* and *his wife*). *They* (option G) is a nominative pronoun that cannot show possession. *Her* (option H) is a singular, female, possessive pronoun, while the sentence needs a plural. *My* (option J) is a possessive pronoun that refers to *I*, or the speaker.

Lesson 3 Practice (page 13)

1. **B** *Their* agrees with the plural noun *Americans*. Option A is not correct because *they* cannot show possession. Option C is not correct because *his* is a singular male pronoun and *Americans* requires a plural pronoun. Option D is not correct because *her* does not agree with *Americans*.

2. **H** Because *difficulty* is not male or female, *it* is the correct pronoun. Options F and G are not correct because they are gender (male or female) pronouns. In option J, the plural pronoun *they* does not agree with the singular noun *difficulty*.

3. **D** *They* agrees with *people*. In option A, the singular pronoun *I* does not agree with the plural noun *people*. In option B, the pronoun *you* does not agree with the plural noun *people*. In option C, *them* is an objective pronoun, which cannot take the place of a subject.

4. **F** The plural pronoun *Their* agrees with the plural nouns *families and individuals*. *They're*, the choice in option G, is not a pronoun. It is a contraction of the words *they are*. Options H and J are singular.

5. **A** *Randall* agrees with *his*. In option B, *her* is not correct, because *sister* and *brother-in-law* require the plural pronoun *them*. In option C, *them* does not agree with *checkbook*, because *them* is plural, and there's only one checkbook. The correct pronoun in this case would be *it*. In option D *him* does not agree with *parents*. The correct plural pronoun in this case would be *them*.

6. **J** The pronoun *it* correctly refers to the noun *trip*. The singular pronoun *she* does not agree with the plural noun *They* in option F. In option G, the plural pronoun *them* does not agree with the singular noun *suitcase*. In option H, *him* is an objective, not a possessive, pronoun. The correct possessive pronoun is *his*.

Lesson 4 Practice (page 15)

1. **B** Both verbs are in the past tense and both actions took place in the past. In option A *check* is incorrect because it is in the present tense. It should be *checked*, because they looked at the recipe *before* they went to the store. In option C, *ask* is in the present tense, and it should be in the past tense to

match *arrived.* In option D, *look* (present tense) should be *looked* (past tense) to match *found.*

2. J Both *helped* and *became* are past tense. This indicates that both actions took place in the past. In option F, *works* is present tense. It should be past tense, *worked,* because the other verb in the sentence, *joined,* is past tense. In option G, *thinks* should be *thought,* because *wanted* is in the past tense. In option H, *learns* should be *learned,* to match the past tense verb *joined.* Both verbs need to be in the past tense.

3. D *Decided* is correct because the action took place at a time in the past. Options A, B, and C are in the present tense.

4. F This sentence requires a past tense verb, since the action took place *one night last week.* Options G, H, and J are all in the present tense.

5. B *Drove* is the correct past tense for the irregular verb *drive.* Options A and D are in the present tense. Option C is an incorrect form of the past tense.

6. H The irregular verb *tell* becomes *told* in the past tense. Option F is an incorrect past tense form. The *–ed* ending is used only on regular verbs. Options G and J are in the present tense.

Lesson 5 Practice (page 17)

1. A The words *next week* mean that the action will take place in the future. That makes *will record* the right answer. Option B is a past tense verb. Options C and D are in the present tense.

2. J The words *When it's done* show that the action will take place in the future. In option F, *send* is in the present tense. In option G, *sended* is an incorrect past tense form of *send,* an irregular verb. Option H is not correct because *sent* is in the past tense. The sentence needs the future tense.

3. C The words *Over the coming six months* indicate that the action will occur in the future. Option A is not correct because it is in the present tense. Options B and D are not correct because they are in the past tense.

4. H The first part of the sentence describes something that may occur in the future. The future tense is needed. That makes *will quit* the right answer. Option F is not correct. *Quitted* is an incorrect form of the past tense. Options G and J are not correct because they are in the present tense.

Lesson 6 Practice (page 19)

1. B The present perfect *(Have)* is the right answer because the action (attending a picnic) is continuing into the present time. *Have* agrees with *I.* Option A is not correct. *Has* does not agree with *I.* *Has* goes with *he, she,* or *it.* Options C (*are*) and D (*did*) are not correct. They are not verbs used with the perfect tenses.

2. J The action, Ron organizing a block picnic, took place *before a known time in the past.* That time was

when he became the planner for this picnic. Option F and option G are not correct. They are both in the present perfect tense. Option H is a verb form that is not used with the perfect tenses.

3. A Option A indicates that the action of printing up a flyer has been *completed.* Options B and C are not correct. They are both verb forms that are not used with the perfect tenses. Option D is not correct. *Has* does not agree with *Ron and his wife Janet.*

4. H This sentence calls for the present perfect tense: *has promised.* The action has been completed at the present time. Option F is in the past perfect tense. Option G does not agree with the subject, *Mr. Green.* In option J, *did* is a verb that is not used with the perfect tenses.

5. A Option A is in the present perfect tense. It indicates that the action of working hard has been completed at the present time. In option B, *have* does not agree with the subject, *weather report.* In option C, *had setting* is not a correct verb form. Option D should be in the past perfect tense: *had been finished.*

6. H The action that the sentence describes, having a terrific time, was completed before a known time in the past. That time was the end of the picnic. Therefore, past perfect is the correct tense. Options F and G should be past perfect, not present perfect. In option J, the verb should be in the present tense, *hope.*

Lesson 7 Practice (page 21)

1. A The subject of this sentence is *workers,* which requires a plural verb. Options B, C, and D are singular.

2. H The subject of this sentence is *owners,* so the verb has to be plural. Don't be misled by the word *factory* in this sentence. It is not the subject. It is the object of the prepositional phrase *of the bolt factory.* Options F, G, and J are not correct. They are all singular.

3. B The subject of this sentence is *Republican and Democratic Parties.* This plural subject needs a plural verb to be in agreement. Options A and C are incorrect because they are singular. Option D is not a complete verb.

4. H This sentence has a plural subject, *Democrats.* Therefore, it needs a plural verb. Options F, G and J are singular.

5. A The singular subject *spending* agrees with the singular verb *was.* In option B, the singular subject *funding* does not agree with the plural verb *were.* In option C, the plural subject *voters* does not agree with the singular verb *was.* In option D, the plural subject *precincts* does not agree with the singular verb *has.*

6. G The plural subject (*members*) agrees with the plural verb (*were reelected*). In option F, the singular subject *referendum* needs a singular verb. In option H, the plural subject *boxes* needs a plural verb. In option J, the singular subject *Election Commissioner Bradley* requires a singular verb.

Lesson 8 Practice (page 23)

1. C In option C, *affect* is correct because the worker's mood can have an influence on how he or she performs the job. In option A, the verb *effected* should be *affected,* meaning "influenced." In option B, the verb should be *affect,* rather than *effect,* because the meaning is "to have an influence on." In option D, the verb should be *effect,* not *affect,* because the political party is trying to bring about change, or "cause it to happen."

2. F Option F correctly uses the verb *teach.* In option G, the verb should be *teach* because the woman from Ford is going to present knowledge to the listeners. In option H, the correct verb should be *teaching,* rather than *learning.* Ms. Schmidt is giving her knowledge to the students. In option J, the verb should be *teach,* which involves gaining knowledge from another person.

3. D Option D correctly uses the verb *accept* which means "to say yes to." In option A, the verb should be *except* not *accept* because *except* means "to leave out." In option B, the verb should be *accepting,* meaning "saying yes to." In option C, the verb should be *accept,* meaning "to say yes to."

4. G Option G correctly uses the verb *lay* to mean "to put or set down." In option F, the verb should be *lie,* because the speaker is talking about placing one's body in a flat position. In options H and J, *lie* should be *lay,* meaning "to put or set down."

5. A In option A, *set* is used correctly, meaning "to put something down." In option B, the verb should be *sit* rather than *set,* because the meaning is "place one's body in a sitting position." In option C, the correct verb is *set.* In option D, *sit* should be *set.*

6. J Option J uses the verb *raise* correctly, meaning "*to lift up.*" In option F, *rise* should be *raise,* meaning "to lift." In option G, the sentence needs the verb *rise,* not *raise.* In option H, the verb should be *raise,* meaning "to lift."

Lesson 9 Practice (page 25)

1. D The superlative is needed because the writer is comparing more than two things. Option A doesn't make a comparison. Option B is an incorrect form of the comparative. Option C compares only two things.

2. F *Cute* is made comparative by adding the ending *–er.* The comparative is needed because the writer is comparing two things: a baby hippo to an adult hippo. Options G and H are incorrect forms of the comparative. Option J does not make a comparison.

3. C This sentence is comparing two things: the time the writer and her family spent at the zoo and the time she wishes they could have spent there. Therefore, the comparative is needed. Option A is not correct because it compares three or more things. Option B

is an incorrect form of the comparative. Option D does not make a comparison.

4. H This sentence needs the superlative. The writer is comparing being a zookeeper to all of the jobs in the world. Option F does not make a comparison. Option G is not correct because it compares only two things. Option J is an incorrect comparative form.

5. A The writer is comparing two jobs—zoo keeping and another job. Therefore, the comparative is right. In option B, *more long* is an incorrect comparative form. Options C compares more than two things. Option D does not make a comparison.

6. J In this sentence, the writer is comparing the job to an office job. Options F and H are not correct comparative forms. Option G is not correct because it compares more than two things.

Lesson 10 Practice (page 27)

1. A This sentence compares two things: how carefully the person is cutting the fish *and* how carefully *he needs to cut it* to filet it successfully. Therefore, option A is the right answer. Option B compares more than two things. Option C does not make a comparison. Option D is not correct because adverbs that end in *–ly* are made comparative by adding the word *more* or *less,* not by changing the ending to *–er.*

2. H This sentence compares two things: when we have to leave and when we had planned to leave. Option F is not correct for two reasons: this adverb does not end in *–ly* or form comparatives with the word *more.* Option G compares more than two things. Option J is not correct because the comparative of *soon* is created only by adding *–er* to the end of the word, not by adding *more* before the word.

3. C This sentence compares two things: how quickly Eddie caught a fish with how quickly John caught a fish. Options A and B are adjectives, not adverbs, and *more* is not used with *–er.* Option D is not correct because the sentence is only comparing two things.

4. G This sentence is comparing two things: how hard Penny tried to catch a fish and how hard John tried to catch a fish. Option F is an incorrect form of an adverb that compares more than two things. Option H is an incorrect comparative because *hard* is made comparative by adding *–er* to the end of the word, not by adding the word *more.* Option J is an incorrect form of the adverb.

5. A This sentence is comparing two things. *Strongly* is an adverb that uses the word *more.* Option B is not correct because the sentence is only comparing two things. Option C is not correct because *more stronger* is an incorrect comparative form. Option D is a comparative adjective, not an adverb, and *most* is used when comparing more than two things.

6. G *More easily* is the correct comparative adverb. In option F, *most easily* is a superlative adverb. Options H and J are incorrect forms of comparative adjectives.

1. D *Glorious* is an adjective that describes *memories.* In option A, *gloriously* is an adverb. Option B is incorrect because it makes a comparison when no comparison needs to be made. Option C is an adverb that compares more than two things.

2. H This sentence needs an adverb to describe *have performed,* the verb. Option F, *mightier,* is a comparative adjective. Option G, *more mighty,* is an incorrect comparative adjective. Option J (*mighty*) is an adjective.

3. B This is an adverb and it describes how Babe Didrikson ran—*successfully. Successfuller* is an incorrect comparative adjective (option A). Option C, *more successful,* is the comparative of the adjective *successful.* Option D, *successful,* is an adjective.

4. F This sentence needs an adjective to describe the sports fans. How were they? *Nervous.* Option G is an adverb that makes a comparison. No comparison is needed. Option H is an incorrect comparative form of the adjective *nervous.* Option J is an adverb.

5. D This sentence is correct as it is written. The adverb describes the way people hoped Hitler would greet the U.S. athletes—*courteously.* Option A is an adjective. Option B is an adjective that makes a comparison. Option C is an adverb that makes a comparison. No comparison is needed.

6. F The adjective *magnificent* describes Jesse Owens, the great athlete. Option G is a comparative adjective and option H is a comparative adverb. These are not correct because no comparison is made in this sentence. Option J is an adverb, while the sentence calls for an adjective.

7. C *Angrily* is an adverb. It describes how Hitler refused to shake Jesse Owens' hand. Options A and B make comparisons, while nothing in this sentence is being compared. Option D is an adjective.

1. B This sentence contains only one negative: *nothing.* The other three sentences are incorrect because each contains two negatives. Option A contains *don't* and *never.* Option C contains *can't* and *nobody.* Option D has the words *didn't* and *no.*

2. G Option G is the only sentence that contains just one negative: *Isn't.* There are two negatives in option F: *couldn't* and *no.* Option H is incorrect as well. It contains two negatives: *don't* and *none.* Option J is not correct because it contains *never* and *nothing.*

3. A Option A contains only one negative: *didn't.* Option B is incorrect because it contains both *didn't* and *nothing.* Option C has *don't* and *no,* and option D has *wasn't* and *no one.*

4. G Option G contains only one negative: *no one.* Option F contains *three* negatives: *didn't, never,* and *nowhere.* Option H has two negatives: *Doesn't* and *nobody.* Option J is not correct because *won't* and *no* are both negatives.

5. C Option C contains only one negative: *didn't.* Option A contains two negatives: *never* and *no.* In option B there are two negatives: *didn't* and *never.* Option D contains the negatives *didn't* and *no.*

6. G In option G there's only one negative: *never.* Option F has two negatives: *hadn't* and *no.* Option H has two negatives: *never* and *no.* Option J has two negatives: *hadn't* and *never.*

1. B *Bad* is an adjective used to describe the noun *voice.* Option A is an adverb that would modify *sounds,* which would not make sense. Option C is an incorrect form of the comparative adjective. No comparison is being made in the sentence. Option D is an incorrect form of the comparative adverb. [Choosing Between Adjectives and Adverbs]

2. F In this sentence, the plural verb *hold* agrees with the plural subject *teachers.* Don't be misled by the word *school,* which comes just before the verb. It is not the subject. It is the object of the prepositional phrase. Option G and H are singular and do not agree with the plural subject *teachers.* Option J is an incorrect form of the verb *hold.* [Subject and Verb Agreement]

3. C This is a nominative pronoun used as the subject of the sentence. Options A, B, and D are not correct because they are objective pronouns and cannot be used to take the place of a subject. [Objective and Nominative Pronouns]

4. G This sentence requires the future tense. Option F is not correct because it is in the past tense. Option H is in the present perfect tense and option J is in the present tense. [Future Tense]

5. A Both verbs are in the past tense. Both actions, seeing the apartment *and* knowing it was perfect, took place at the same time in the past. Option B is not correct because *becomes* is present tense. It should be *became,* the past tense. Option C (*will rent*) is in the future tense, while the words *last week* signal that the verb should be *rented,* the past tense. Option D uses the past tense incorrectly. *Sent* should be *send,* because the action will take place in the future. [Past Tense]

6. J Option J correctly uses the comparative adverb. Because *quickly* ends in *–ly,* it is correct to use *more.* Option F contains *more loud,* an incorrect form of the comparative adjective. It should contain the comparative adverb, *more loudly.* In option G, adverbs do not use both *more* and *–er* to make their comparative. In option H, *fastest* should be *faster* because the sentence is comparing only two things. [Comparative Adverbs]

7. B In option B *their* agrees with its antecedent, *children.* Both are plural. In option A the subject, *parent,* needs a singular pronoun. *Their* is not correct and should be *his* or *her* (either one is correct). In option C, the noun *chemical* needs a singular pronoun in the second part of the sentence. *Them,* plural, should be *it,* singular. In option D, *chemicals,* a plural noun, needs a plural pronoun in the second part of the sentence. *It* is singular. The correct pronoun is *them.* [Antecedent Agreement]

8. **H** *Raise* is the correct verb because it means "to lift something up." In option F *set,* which means "to put something down," should be used in this sentence. Option G's verb should be *raise,* which means "to lift something up." *Rise* means "to stand up or to move up automatically." In option J, *learned* is not correct. It means "to gain knowledge yourself." The correct verb is *taught,* the past tense of *teach. Teach* means "to help someone else gain knowledge." [Easily Confused Verbs]

9. **B** Option B is correct because the sentence needs a past tense plural verb. The time when women could not vote is in the past, and the verb must be plural because *women* is the plural of *woman.* In option A, *are* is plural and in the present tense. In option C, *is* is singular and in the present tense. Option D is singular and in the past tense. [Past Tense]

10. **F** Option F is the only option that does not contain two negatives. It has only one—*no.* Option G contains two *(never* and *no).* Option H contains two *(hadn't* and *no).* Option J has two negatives *(didn't* and *no).* [Using Negatives]

11. **D** Option D correctly uses the objective plural pronoun *them* as the object of the prepositional phrase *of them.* Option A and option B are both nominative pronouns, which are used to take the place of a subject. Option C is a singular objective pronoun. The sentence needs a plural pronoun because the pronoun refers to *suffragists.* [Objective and Nominative Pronouns]

12. **G** The comparative is needed because the sentence compares two things: how hard the suffragists struggled before setbacks and how hard they struggled after setbacks. Option F is an incorrect form of the comparative adverb. Option H is an adverb that compares more than two things. Option J is an incorrect form of the comparative adverb. Short adverbs do not use both *more* and the *–er* ending to form their comparatives. [Comparative and Superlative Adverbs]

13. **C** Option C is the comparative of the adjective *courageous.* The writer is comparing two things: Carrie Chapman Catt *and* all other women as a single group. Because *courageous* is a longer adjective, use the word *more* rather than the ending *–er.* Option A is a comparative adverb. Option B does not make a comparison. Option D compares more than two things. [Comparative and Superlative Adjectives]

14. **G** This sentence requires a possessive pronoun that agrees with the subject, *women. Women* is plural; therefore *their* is the correct choice. Option F is a nominative pronoun that cannot show possession. Option H is a singular possessive pronoun and does not agree with the plural *women.* Option J is an

objective pronoun, which cannot show possession. [Possessive and Relative Pronouns]

Lesson 13 Practice (page 35)

1. **C** This is the only choice that has both a subject and a verb and is not a run-on sentence. *Melinda and Paul* is the subject. *Chose* is the verb. Option A is a fragment without a subject. Who is choosing a family doctor? Option B needs a verb. Option D is a run-on sentence. The two sentences that are incorrectly joined are *They chose a new doctor* and *She's from Pakistan.*

2. **F** This choice has both a subject *(One)* and a verb *(was born).* Option G is a run-on sentence. *They have two children* and *one is only four months old* are incorrectly joined together. Option H is a fragment without a subject. Option J is a fragment and needs a verb.

3. **C** *When they arrived* is a fragment if it is not joined to the first sentence. The complete correct sentence, *The emergency room was very crowded when Paul and Melinda arrived,* has a subject *(room)* and a verb *(was).* In option A *when Paul and Melinda arrived* is still a fragment, this time without a capital letter. In option B the same fragment is still in the paragraph and the word *crowded* incorrectly begins with a capital letter. Option D is not correct, as *When Paul and Melinda arrived* is a fragment.

4. **J** The sentence is correct as it is. It has a subject *(They)* and a verb *(breathed).* Option F contains a fragment, *When the nurse called their name.* Option G is a fragment, lacking a verb. Option H is missing the word *when.*

Lesson 14 Practice (page 37)

1. **C** Option C is the best sentence combination because it joins the adverbs *proudly* and *expertly* from Sentences 2 and 3 into a phrase with the conjunction *and* and inserts the phrase into Sentence 1. Option A unnecessarily repeats the subject and verb. Option B unnecessarily alters the direct sentence order and uses a comma. Option D leaves out the phrase *in the parade.*

2. **F** Option F supplies all the information from both sentences, but repeats nothing. Option G repeats *Malcolm.* Option H repeats *visited.* Option J repeats *job counselor.*

3. **B** Option B combines all the information from the two sentences and leaves nothing out. Option A leaves out the information that the trees were cut down to make room for the highway. Options C and D both repeat *trees.*

4. **G** In option F, the adverb *loudly* is missing. In option H, the adjective *big* is missing. In option J, *this morning* is missing.

1. **A** Option A combines the subjects and states the verb just once. Option B is difficult to understand. What did Charlie do along with his neighbor? Option C repeats *filled out*. Option D repeats many words.

2. **G** Option G combines the subjects and states the verb just once. Option F leaves out *of the form*, making the sentence hard to understand. Option H repeats *of the form* unnecessarily. Option J repeats many words.

3. **B** Option B combines the subjects and states the verb just once. Option A suggests that contractors can install dealers. Option C changes the meaning of the sentences. Option D repeats many words.

4. **F** Option F combines the subjects and states the verb just once. Options G and H do not repeat words, but they change the meaning of the original sentences. Option J repeats too many words.

1. **B** In option B, the two sentences are combined without repeating, changing, or leaving out any information. In option A, the meaning of the original sentences is changed. Option C is confusing: *Many people* and *other people* are not clear. Option D repeats *people* and *music* and adds the unnecessary word *too*.

2. **H** Option H includes all the information in both sentences. In option F, the information that the speaker likes cooking hamburgers on a grill is left out. Option G is a run-on sentence because it does not include *and*. In option J, the information from the second sentence is stated first, which makes the meaning of the new sentence confusing.

3. **C** Option C correctly includes the word *but* to join the two sentences and also uses the nominative pronoun *she*. In option A, *mail* is repeated. In option B, *the mail carrier* is repeated. Option D includes incorrect information, because it says the speaker asked the carrier to leave the mail in the box on the porch bench.

4. **H** This option supplies all the necessary information. It leaves out unnecessary repetition of information. In option F, *the teachers enjoy teaching* is repeated, and in option G, *at our school* is repeated. In option J, the meaning of the sentences changes.

5. **A** This option correctly includes *but* to join the two sentences and does not leave out or change any information. In option B, the order of the sentences is reversed, which confuses the meaning. In option C, *when she left* is in the wrong place. It should follow *door*. Option D is a run-on sentence because it does not include *but* to join the two sentences.

6. **G** Option G joins the sentences with *and* and includes all the information. Option F is a run-on sentence. Option H is a run-on and it repeats *hundreds of people*. In option J, *the show* is repeated.

1. **B** It is clear in this option B that Jenny, not her dad, is the one who was 12 at the time her dad remarried. Option A is a run-on sentence. Option C is not correct because it says that Jenny's dad was 12 when he remarried. In option D, it is unclear who was 12, Jenny or her dad.

2. **F** Option F makes it clear that the snowflakes are falling gently outside the window. In option G, the words *falling gently outside the window* immediately follow *We,* which gives the sentence the meaning that the speaker and his wife were falling outside the window. In option H, the words *of the year* are incorrectly separated from the word they describe, *snowflakes.* In option J, it is not clear what is falling gently outside the window.

3. **D** It is clear that *with a beautiful voice* should follow and describe *A soloist.* Option A contains a sentence fragment, *A few songs,* and is therefore incorrect. Option B is not correct because *with a beautiful voice* follows *songs.* The songs don't have the beautiful voice; the singer does. Option C includes a sentence fragment, *Sang a few songs.*

4. **H** In option H, it is clear that the speaker and his wife saw the wedding cake as they were walking past the food table. Including *We* and *it* as subjects helps make the sentence clear. In option F, the wedding cake is looking delicious and walking past the table. In option G the cake is walking. In option J it is not clear what is walking.

5. **A** Placing *with a great saxophone player* right after *band* leaves no doubt that it's the band that has the great horn player. In option B, the words *with a great saxophone player* follow *music.* This word order means that the music has a great saxophone player, not the band. Option C includes a sentence fragment. In option D, *with a great saxophone player* follows *dancing.* This word order means that people at the wedding were *dancing with* a great saxophone player.

6. **G** In this choice, the word *almost* is placed next to *midnight.* This means that the speaker and his wife stayed at the reception until about 11:45 p.m. In option F, it is unclear what the word *almost* refers to. In option H, it is not clear what the sentence means because the placement of *almost* is very confusing. In option J, *almost* is next to *stayed,* rather than to *midnight.* Therefore, the meaning is that the speaker almost stayed at the reception, but then didn't, for some reason.

1. **D** In this option, two similar parts of the sentence, *tearing down* and *rebuilding,* are both in –*ing* form. In option A, *tearing down* and *when they rebuild* are not in the same form. In option B, *tearing down* and *to rebuild* are not in the same form. In option C, *to tear down* and *rebuilding* are not in the same form.

2. G In this option *helping the adults* and *lending a hand* are in the same *–ing* form. In option F, *helping* and *lend* are not in the same form. In option H, *when they help* and *lending* do not have the same form. In option J, *to help* and *lending* do not match.

3. A Option A is the only choice with *measuring* and *cutting* in a matching form. In option B, *measuring* and *to cut* are not in the same form. In option C, *to measure* and *cutting* do not match. In option D, *measuring* and *cut* do not match.

4. G *Sawing, hammering,* and *picking up trash* all use the *–ing* form. Option F is not correct because it includes the word *to* before *sawing*. In option H *to saw, hammer,* and *picking up trash* do not match. In option J, *hammer* does not match *sawing* and *picking up*.

5. C Option C is the only option in which *fixing* and *bringing* are in the same form. In option A, *fixing* does not match *bring*. In option B, *to fix* and *bringing* do not match. In option D, *fixing food* and *when they bring snacks and drinks* do not match.

6. G *Singing* and *praying* are both in the *–ing* form, making this option the correct one. In option F, *singing* and *when they pray* do not match. In option H, *singing* and *pray* are not in the same form. In option J, *sing* and *praying* do not match.

TABE Review: Sentence Formation (page 46)

1. D This choice has a subject *(you)* and a verb *(receive)*. Option A has no subject. Option B also has no subject. Option C has no verb. [Sentence Recognition]

2. F In option F the adjective *red* is placed in front of the word it modifies, *barn*. Option G repeats *is*. Option H includes three unnecessary words, *is, and,* and *it*. Option J includes three unnecessary words and an unnecessary comma. [Adding Modifiers to Combine Sentences]

3. D Option D combines the two sentences by combining the two subjects *(farming* and *mining)* using *and*. Because the subject of the combined sentence is plural, the sentence needs *are,* rather than *is*. In this option, *business* is changed to *businesses* because of the change from singular to plural. In option A, *is an important business in our area* is repeated. Option B is a run-on sentence because it does not use *and* to join the sentences. In option C the subjects are combined and made plural but the singular *is* does not change to the plural *are*. [Compounding]

4. F In option F, the coordinating conjunction *but* is used to combine the two sentences without leaving out, repeating, or changing any information. In option G, the order of the two sentences is reversed, making it unclear what *Some* refers to. In option H, *some* is placed before *farmers,* which changes the sentence to read that *some* farmers are injured and *some others* are careful. Option J is a run-on sentence because it does not use *but* to join the two original sentences. [Coordinating]

5. C In option C, *working* and *being* have parallel structure. In option A, *working* and *to be* do not match. In option B, *to work* and *being* do not match. In option D, *working* and *when they can be* do not match. [Nonparallel Structure]

6. F In option F, *sitting on a tractor* and *looking out over their fields* follows *Farmers,* the word the phrases describe. In option G, it is unclear whether the fields or the farmer is sitting on the tractor. Option H has the same problem because *sitting on a tractor* follows *fields,* not *Farmers*. Option J is also confusing. *Sitting on a tractor* again follows *fields,* rather than *farmers*. [Misplaced Modifiers]

Lesson 19 Practice (page 48)

1. A This paragraph discusses ways that sheep are valuable to people, making option A the right choice. Options B and D focus on a single product that we get from sheep. Option C is incorrect because the paragraph does not discuss why sheep are misunderstood.

2. J This paragraph gives answers to the question of why basketball is popular, making J correct. The paragraph says nothing about particular players, making option F incorrect. Option G is incorrect because the paragraph does not compare basketball and baseball. Option H, while true, does not serve as a good introduction to the paragraph.

3. C This choice is correct because the paragraph describes how different languages use "son of" in family names. Option A is not as specific about the subject of the paragraph. Options B and D are incorrect because they focus on how individual families treat their children, rather than how different languages treat names.

4. G This paragraph compares Mexico and Canada, so option G is correct. Option F is incorrect because the paragraph does not discuss the United States or state that one country is better than another. Option H makes a statement about climates, which the paragraph does not discuss. Option J, while true, does not introduce the main subject of the paragraph.

Lesson 20 Practice (page 50)

1. B This choice explains why Chavez was a hero. Option A is about Martin Luther King, Jr. Option C describes the lives of farm workers, but does not explain what Chavez did for them. Option D is about Mexican Americans.

2. H Option H gives reasons and examples why the writer believes working a night shift can be good for some people. Option F discusses being prompt on the job, instead of night-shift work. Option B explains some of the problems, rather than benefits of night work. Option J lists different night-shift jobs.

3. A This choice is correct because it explains some of the challenges of retirement saving and what some people may be forced to do in response to these challenges. Option B is about checking accounts. Option C is about the challenges facing single parents, not about retirement savings. Option D describes how some other countries address pensions and retirement.

Lesson 21 Practice (page 52)

1. D The missing piece of information is that the coach stopped the game by calling timeout. Options A, B, and C all give useful information. However, they do not explain how the game stopped or how the players came to be sitting on the bench.

2. J This paragraph needs an explanation of what the children did between the time they got dressed and the time they came home. Option J is the only sentence that gives this information. Options F, G, and H give information that is probably true. However, none of these choices supplies the needed information.

3. C The writer has left out the step of putting the popcorn in the pan. It's the only answer that fits in this location in the paragraph. Option A is a necessary step, but it is a step that would fit into the second sentence, not after the second sentence. Option B is a step that has already been completed. You would not buy the popcorn after you heat the oil in the pan. Option D is good advice, but it doesn't fit, either.

4. F This paragraph needs a sentence that tells that the sun has disappeared. Only option F gives this information. Option G belongs earlier in the paragraph, as the sun is setting. Option H describes what the view is like after the sun has gone down. Option J belongs at the beginning of the paragraph, as a topic sentence.

Lesson 22 Practice (page 54)

1. B The main topic of the paragraph is Thanksgiving. Sentence 2 gives information about the Pilgrims before they came to Massachusetts, which is interesting, but not directly related to the main topic. Options A, C, and D relate to the main topic.

2. H The main topic of the paragraph is Justin and his father's new computer. Sentence 3 is unrelated to the main topic. Options F, G, and J relate to the main topic.

3. D Option D is an interesting detail about small towns, but it is not related to the main topic. The main topic of the paragraph is that many people prefer small-town life. Options A, B, and C offer reasons why the writer believes that people prefer small-town life.

4. F Option F is a topic sentence that is not related to the rest of the paragraph. It makes a statement about people's eating habits. Options G, H, and J discuss three different root vegetables.

1. A This option gives reasons why it is important to know how to change a tire. Option B describes different kinds of tires, not why knowing how to change them is important. Option C is about another kind of emergency. Option D is about organizations that provide help, not why knowing how to change your own tire is a good idea. [Supporting Sentences]

2. H The paragraph is about how different people define success. Option H is the only choice that fits this topic. Option F is about why success is hard to find, not how people define it. Options G and J state judgments about what makes a person successful. They do not introduce the subject of how different people define success. [Topic Sentence]

3. D The paragraph needs a sentence that says the hardware store was on fire. Option A, while true, does not explain why the fire trucks were there. Option B should come before the first sentence because it explains why Jan went to the hardware store in the first place. Option C belongs at the end. It's what Jan did after finding that the hardware store was on fire. [Sequence]

4. H The third sentence is a general statement about employment agencies and how they can help people find jobs. It has nothing to do with the main topic, adjusting to a new job. Options F, G, and J are directly related to the main topic. [Unrelated Sentences]

Lesson 23 Practice (page 57)

1. A *Thanksgiving* (a holiday), *Thursday* (a day of the week), and *November* (a month) are all correctly capitalized in this option. In option B *Month* should not be capitalized. *Tower* and *State* should not be capitalized in option C. *Theater* and *Movie* are incorrectly capitalized in option D.

2. H Other than the first word, *Tuesday* is the only word in this sentence that should be capitalized. In option F, *third,* part of the name of the street, should be capitalized. *Summer* should not be capitalized in option G. *Daughter* should not be capitalized in option J.

3. B *Lassie* and *Timmy* are correctly capitalized in this choice. In option A, *the beatles,* the name of the music group, should be capitalized. In option C, *Morning* should not be capitalized. In option D, *Book* is incorrectly capitalized.

4. G *Montgomery Journal* is correctly capitalized in this option. In option F, *Ad* should not be capitalized and *journal* should be. In option H, *Montgomery Journal* should be capitalized. In option J, *journal,* part of the name of the newspaper, should be capitalized.

5. C This option includes capital letters starting the words *Ms., Antoinette, Mitchell,* and *She.* In option A *ms.* should be capitalized. In option B, *mitchell,* the woman's last name, should be capitalized. In option

D, *she* should be capitalized because it is the first letter of the fourth sentence in the paragraph.

6. J In option J, *Friday* and *Lonnie* are correctly capitalized. In option F, *Week* is incorrectly capitalized. In option G, *lonnie* should be capitalized. Option H is not correct because *Week* should not be capitalized and *friday* should be capitalized.

Lesson 24 Practice (page 59)

1. C Option C is a statement and requires a period. It does not show strong feelings (option A), and it is not a question (option B). However, it is a complete sentence, so it requires an end mark (option D).

2. G This sentence is a question. It does not show strong feelings (option F) and is not a statement (option H). It is a complete sentence, so it requires an end mark (option J).

3. A This quotation expresses strong feelings, so the sentence requires an exclamation point. The quotation is not a question (option B). It is a complete sentence, so it requires an end mark in addition to the quotation marks (option C). A period is not correct here (option D).

4. F Although option F includes a quotation with an exclamation point, the whole sentence is a statement, so it requires a period. It is not a question (option G). This part of the sentence is not a quotation that expresses strong feelings (option H). An exclamation point is incorrect here (option J).

5. B Option B is a statement that does not express strong feelings, so it ends with a period. Options A, C, and D are also all statements that should end with periods.

6. J This sentence expresses strong feelings, so it ends correctly with an exclamation point. Options F and G are statements and should end with periods. Option H is a question and requires a question mark.

Lesson 25 Practice (page 61)

1. C In option C the comma is correctly placed before *Al*, who is being addressed directly. In option A, the direct address comma is omitted. In option B, there is an unnecessary comma after *look*. In option D, the direct address comma before *Al* is missing and there is an unnecessary comma after *look*.

2. G Option G correctly includes a comma between *Atlanta* and *Georgia*. In option F, there is comma at the end of the sentence, rather than a period. In option H, the comma is incorrectly placed after *store*. In option J, the comma is incorrectly placed before *Atlanta*.

3. A The compound sentence should be separated with a comma before *but*. Therefore, Options B, C, and D are incorrect.

4. F Because it lists a series of three things that Barbara did, the sentence needs a series comma after *breath*. Therefore, options G, H, and J are not correct.

TABE Review: Capitalization and Punctuation (page 62)

1. A This sentence requires a comma after *Reggie* because he is being addressed directly by the speaker. Option B is incorrect because the sentence is a statement, not an expression of strong emotion. Option C is also incorrect because the sentence is not a question. [Commas]

2. H This sentence is a question. Therefore, a question mark is the correct end mark. It also has a comma between the two parts of the compound sentence. Option F is not correct because the sentence is a question, not a statement. Option G is not correct because the sentence has no need for an additional comma. Option J is not correct because the sentence needs an end mark. [End Marks]

3. B Option A is not correct because it has a comma after *and*. Option C is incorrect because it has a comma after *and,* and it lacks one after *planers*. Option D is missing the series comma after *planers*. [Commas]

4. H Option F is not correct because the first word should be capitalized. Option G is not correct because *october* and *burt* should be capitalized and *Brother* and *Law* should not be capitalized. Option J is not correct because *brother* and *law* should not be capitalized, and *October* and *Last* should be capitalized. [Capitalization]

5. B In option B, the city and state names are capitalized and the commas are used correctly. In option A, *Highway* is incorrectly capitalized. Option C is not correct because the first word of the sentence should be capitalized. In option D, *cole* should be capitalized. [Capitalization]

6. J This sentence is a statement and ends with a period. Option F should end with a question mark. Option G is a statement and should not end with an exclamation point. Option H is a statement, not a question. [End Marks]

Lesson 26 Practice (page 64)

1. B There should be quotation marks before *Dinner* because this is where the butler's exact words begin. Options A, C, and D are incorrect.

2. J This sentence is correct as it is written. There is a comma following *shouted,* quotation marks around the exact words spoken, and an exclamation point at the end, inside the quotation marks. Options F, G, and H are not correct.

3. B This sentence has quotation marks around the woman's exact words, a comma inside the quotation marks, and a period at the end of the sentence. In option A, quotation marks should enclose *Was that a shot?* In option C, the quotation mark before the first *I* is omitted. In option D, the comma inside the quotation marks following *sofa* is omitted. Option D also incorrectly includes a period after *Stoycheff*.

4. H This sentence has a comma after *out* and quotation marks around *Sir Andrew has been murdered!* Option F is not correct because the final period is outside the quotation marks. It also needs a comma after *said.* In option G, *A gasp* should not have quotation marks around it because they are not someone's exact words. In option J, the quotation marks after *Oh* and before the first *I* are omitted.

5. C In option C there is a comma after *gentlemen* and before the quotation marks. In option A the quotation mark should come after the comma following *gentlemen,* rather than at the end of the sentence. Option B includes a period rather than a comma after *gentlemen.* In option D, there should be a comma between *gentlemen* and the quotation marks.

6. F Option F has a comma after *added* rather than a period. In option G, there is an incorrectly placed period after *here.* Option G also has no comma after *added,* and no quotation mark before *and.* In option H there should be quotation marks after the comma following *here* and a comma instead of a period after *added.* Option J is not correct because there is a period after *added.* It should be a comma.

1. A This option includes a correctly placed apostrophe to show ownership. In option B, the apostrophe is incorrectly placed after the *s.* In option C, there should be no apostrophe in *friend's.* In option D, there should be an apostrophe in *Daniels.*

2. G This choice correctly places the apostrophe in *he'd,* a contraction of "he would." Option F has an incorrect apostrophe in *friend's.* The apostrophe in the contraction of "he would" is in the wrong place in option H and is missing in option J.

3. C *Restaurant's* is the only word in the sentence that needs an apostrophe. It needs it to show ownership. Option A is not correct because it includes an apostrophe in *planners.* In option B, the apostrophe in *restaurants'* is in the wrong place. In option D, the apostrophe is missing.

4. J This option correctly includes the apostrophe in *daughter's.* Option F omits the possessive apostrophe in *cars.* Option G omits the apostrophe in the contraction of "I would." In option H, there should be a possessive apostrophe in *stores.*

5. A In this choice, the apostrophe in *I'm,* a contraction of "I am," is correct. In option B, the apostrophe in the contraction of "you are" is misplaced. In option C, there should be an apostrophe in *moms.* In option D, there should be an apostrophe in *friends.*

6. H The apostrophe in *we'll,* a contraction of "we will," is correct. In option F, the possessive apostrophe that belongs before the *s* in *Rudys* is missing. In option G, the apostrophe in the contraction of "it is" is in the wrong place. In option J, the apostrophe in the contraction of "she is" is missing.

1. B In this choice, *April* is capitalized and there is a comma after *12.* In option A, the comma that belongs after *12* is omitted. Option C places the comma after *April,* not after *12.* In option D, *april* should be capitalized.

2. F In option F, *P* and *O* and *Box* are correctly capitalized. Option G is not correct because *p and o* and *box* should be capitalized. In option H, *box* should be capitalized, and in option J, *p* and *o* should be capitalized.

3. C The complete name of the road is capitalized. Option A includes an incorrect comma after *5670.* In option B, *newcastle* and *road* should be capitalized, and in option D, *road* should be capitalized.

4. G In this choice, *Richmond* and *Indiana* are capitalized, and *Richmond* is followed by a comma. In option F, *indiana* should be capitalized, and in option H, *richmond* should be capitalized. Option J includes an incorrect comma after *Indiana.*

5. D This salutation is correct as it is written. All the words are capitalized, and it ends with a colon. In option A, the colon is missing. In option B, *dear* should be capitalized, and in option C, *personnel* should be capitalized.

6. H In option H, *Yours* begins with a capital letter, *truly* does not, and a comma follows *truly.* Option F is incorrect because *Truly* should not be capitalized. Option G is missing a comma and *Truly* is capitalized, and in option J, *yours* should be capitalized.

1. A This sentence needs a question mark before the second quotation marks, because Mark's exact words form a question. Option B is incorrect because both sets of quotation marks are already in the sentence. Option C is incorrect because Mark's words are not a statement, but a question. Option D is incorrect because there must be a question mark at the end of Mark's words. [Quotation Marks]

2. H In option H, the apostrophe is included in the contraction of "She is." Option F is not correct because *familys'* should be *family's,* to show ownership. Option G is incorrect because the second quotation marks should follow *up,* to enclose her exact words. Option J is incorrect because the apostrophe in the contraction of "had not" is missing. [Apostrophes]

3. D The contraction *won't,* for "will not," correctly includes the apostrophe. In option A, there should be a comma, not a period, after *said.* In option B, the apostrophe that belongs in *Sandies* is missing. In option C, there should be quotation marks at the beginning of Vern's exact words. [Apostrophes]

4. H *November* is capitalized, and there is a comma after 15. In option F, the comma is omitted, while in option G, *november* should be capitalized. Option J is incorrect because the comma follows *November,* not *15.* [Parts of a Letter]

5. D In option D, *Main* and *Street* begin with capital letters. In option A, *main* and *street* should be capitalized. In option B, *street* should be capitalized, and in option C, *main* should be capitalized. [Parts of a Letter]

6. G In option G, *Wakefield* and *Rhode Island* begin with capital letters, and *Wakefield* is followed by a comma. Option F is incorrect because *rhode* should be capitalized. In option H, there is an incorrect comma after *Island.* In option J, the comma after *Wakefield* is missing. [Parts of a Letter]

TABE Review: Spelling (page 73–74)

1. D The "uh" sound in this word's second syllable is spelled with an *e.* Options A, B, and C are misspelled. [Vowels]

2. F In this word, the ending *–ion* is added to the root *possess* without any changes to the root. Options G, H, and J are misspelled. [Structural Units]

3. C In the word *transfer,* double the *r* before adding the *–ed* ending that makes it past tense. Options A, B, and D are misspelled. [Consonants]

4. H *Scenery* has a silent letter—the *c.* Options F and G are misspelled. Option J is incorrect. *Scenery* has three syllables. [Consonants]

5. B The first three vowels in this word are short vowels, while the final *e* is silent. Options A, C, and D are misspelled. [Vowels]

6. H The *c* in *sincere* is pronounced like an *s.* In addition, the vowel sound in the second syllable is pronounced like the sound in *fear* or *hear.* Options F, G, and J are misspelled. [Vowels]

7. B The *y* in *happy* changes to an *i* when the suffix *–ness* is added. Options A, C, and D are misspelled. [Structural Units]

8. H The *j* sound in *soldiers* is a variant spelling, in this case spelled with the letter *d.* Options F, G, and J are misspelled. [Consonants]

9. A The long vowel sound in *season* is spelled with the *ea* letter combination. Options B, C, and D are misspelled. [Vowels]

10. J This word ends in *–ous.* Options F, G, and H are misspelled. [Structural Units]

11. C Option C is the correct spelling. Option A is a homonym. Options B and D are misspellings. [Structural Units]

12. F The *t* in *advantage* is often silent, although some people may pronounce it. Options G, H, and J are misspelled. [Silent Letter Consonants]

13. D The long *a* sound in this word is spelled with the letter combination *ai.* This word also has a silent letter, the *g.* Options A, B, and C are misspelled. [Vowels]

14. G The "uh" sound in the third syllable of this word is a schwa. Here it is correctly spelled with an *a.* In

addition, the short vowel sound of the second syllable is spelled with an *e.* Options F, H, and J are misspelled. [Vowels]

15. D Doubling a consonant does not change the way it's pronounced. Options A and C do not double the consonant *p.* Option B has the wrong vowel. [Vowels]

16. H The *c* in *recipe* sounds like an *s.* Options F, G, and J are misspelled. [Consonants]

17. A Long vowels have a longer sound. Some long vowel sounds are spelled with a combination of letters. Options B, C, and D are misspelled. [Vowels]

18. G The vowels in the word are short vowels. There is no need for a double consonant (options H and J). Option F is misspelled. [Consonants]

19. D The "uh" sound is spelled with an *o.* The *e* is a short vowel. Options A, B, and C are misspelled. [Vowels]

Performance Assessment Language

Sample Items (page 75)

A. A This sentence is correct in the present tense. Option B is a sentence fragment. Option C should be future tense, as indicated by *tomorrow.* Option D should have a pronoun that can be used as an object: *them,* rather than *they.*

B. J Option J is a statement, and it correctly ends with a period. Option F has no end mark. In option G, *saturday* should be capitalized. Option H should end with a question mark.

C. C Option C combines the two sentences without leaving out, adding, or changing the information in the original sentences. In option A, it is unclear what is juicy. In option B, the adjective *juicy* is changed to a verb, *juiced.* Option D uses extra unnecessary words.

D. H Option H has a question mark at the end of the first sentence and a capital letter at the beginning of the second sentence. In option F, the first sentence should end with a question mark. In option G, there is a comma where there should be a period, and the first word of the second sentence should be capitalized. In option J, the first word of the second sentence is not capitalized.

(page 76)

1. D This sentence makes a comparison, so the comparative adverb *sooner* is correct. Options A and B are incorrect comparative forms. Option C is used for comparing more than two things. [Comparative Adverbs]

2. H Because *dog* is singular, a singular verb is needed. Options F, G, and J are plural. [Subject and Verb Agreement]

3. B This sentence calls for the present perfect tense. Options A, C, and D are not used with the perfect tenses. [Perfect Tense]

4. H Option H combines the sentences using *but* without repeating, changing, or leaving out information.

Options F, G, and J all have different meanings than the original sentences. [Coordinating]

5. **A** Option A combines the sentences without changing the meaning of the original sentences or repeating any information. In option B, the *mall*, not the *DVD player*, is described as new. Option C places the modifier *that Jill bought* too far from *DVD player*. In option D, *DVD player* is repeated. [Adding Modifiers to Combine Sentences]

(page 77)

6. **J** In this option, *washing machine* and *dryer* is a compound subject, and the plural verb matches. In option F *in the basement* is repeated, and in option G, *is* is a singular verb. Option H leaves out *and* and incorrectly uses a comma. [Compounding]

7. **A** In option A, *Sandie, Rose, and Thomas* is a compound subject joined by *and* with series commas. In option B, the meaning of the sentence is changed. In options C and D, *went to the football game* is repeated. [Compounding]

8. **H** In option F, *completed* is repeated. In options G and J, the adverbs are changed to adjectives. [Adding Modifiers to Combine Sentences]

9. **C** Sentences 1, 2, and 4 discuss the problem of low voter participation in the United States. Sentence 3 is about voting machines. [Unrelated Sentence]

10. **F** Sentences 2, 3, and 4 are about the Statue of Liberty. Sentence 1 is about Ellis Island, which is near the Statue of Liberty, but an entirely different subject. [Unrelated Sentence]

(page 78)

11. **D** Because *new* is a short word, adding the *–er* ending is the correct way to make a comparison. Option A is an incorrect form of an adjective. Options B and C include *more*, which should only be used to form the comparative of multi-syllable adjectives. [Comparative and Superlative Adjectives]

12. **G** Both the name of the place, *Denali National Park*, and the state, *Alaska*, should be capitalized. In option F, *denali* should be capitalized. In option H, *In* is incorrectly capitalized. In option J, *alaska* should be capitalized. [Capitalization]

13. **B** The past tense is correct in this sentence. Options A and C are present tense. Option D is future tense. [Past Tense]

14. **H** *Them* is a plural pronoun that serves as the object and refers to *parks*. In option F, *it* is singular and does not agree with plural *parks*. Option G is incorrect because *him* is singular and male. Option J should only be used as the subject, not the object, of a sentence. [Objective and Nominative Pronouns]

(page 79)

15. **A** In option A, the month is capitalized and a comma follows the day. In option B *june* should be capitalized. In option C, the comma that should follow the day is missing. In option D, the comma is misplaced after *June*. [Parts of a Letter]

16. **J** In option F, *high* should be capitalized, and in option G, *street* should be capitalized. Option H includes an unnecessary comma. [Parts of a Letter]

17. **B** In option B, the city and state names are capitalized, and there is a comma following the city. Option A has an extra comma. Options C and D are incorrectly capitalized. [Parts of a Letter]

18. **F** In option F, each word begins with a capital letter, *Dr.*, the abbreviation for *Doctor*, is followed by a period, and the salutation ends with a colon. In option G, *dear and dr.* should be capitalized. In option H, the semicolon should be a colon. In option J, the abbreviation for doctor should end with a period. [Parts of a Letter]

19. **B** Both words in the title of the newspaper should begin with capital letters. In option A, *seattle* should be capitalized. In option C, both *seattle* and *weekly* should be capitalized. In option D, *weekly* should be capitalized. [Capitalization]

20. **J** Option J correctly uses *my* to show ownership. Option F an objective pronoun. Options G and H are incorrect pronoun forms. [Possessive and Relative Pronouns]

21. **C** The future tense is correct, as indicated by *next week*. Option A is past tense, option B is present perfect tense, and option D is an incorrect verb form. [Future Tense]

(page 80)

22. **F** The first word of the second sentence should begin with a capital *I*. In option G, the first sentence ends with a comma. In option H, a period should follow *countries* and the second sentence should begin with a capital letter. In option J, *in* should be capitalized. [Capitalization]

23. **D** Option D includes commas after *Italy*, *Germany*, and *Canada*. Option A lacks a comma after *Italy*, while option B has an extra comma after *Great*. In option C, there is an unnecessary comma after *and*. [Commas]

24. **H** An adverb is needed to modify the verb *has increased*. Options G and J are adjectives. Option F is an incorrect comparative form of *great*. [Choosing Between Adjectives and Adverbs]

25. **B** Names of countries are always capitalized. In options C and D, not all country names are capitalized. In option A, *and* is incorrectly capitalized. [Capitalization]

26. **H** In option H, both activities have the same *–ing* form. In option F, there is only one verb. In option G *work* does not match *getting*. In option J, *working* does not match *get*. [Nonparallel Structure]

27. **B** Option B is a relative pronoun that connects the two parts of the sentence. Options A and C are pronouns that are used with people, not with things. Option D is an incorrect relative pronoun. [Possessive and Relative Pronouns]

28. **J** *Daylight Savings Time* is singular, so the verb *was* is correct. Options F and G are plural, while option H is an incorrect verb form. [Subject and Verb Agreement]

29. **C** Because *states* is plural, the plural possessive pronoun *their* is correct. Option A is singular, and option B should be used as the object of a sentence. Option D is plural, but it is the kind of pronoun that should be used as the subject of a sentence. [Antecedent Agreement]

30. **J** In option J, the series comma is used correctly. In option F, a comma should follow *Hawaii*. In option G, there is an unnecessary comma after *part*. In option H, the comma is after *and* when it should be after *Hawaii*. [Commas]

31. **A** Option A gives a reason why the topic sentence is true and explains where future health care workers will find employment. In option B, the subject is why people avoid going to the doctor and the problems this causes. Option C is about one particular health problem, and option D is about unemployment over different time periods. [Supporting Sentences]

32. **G** Option G is about the five military branches. It describes some ways in which they are different. Option F focuses only on two of the branches. Option H is about veterans, not the branches of the military. Option J lists three of the branches in order of size, but does not mention the other two branches. [Supporting Sentences]

33. **C** The speaker is making a direct address, so there should be a comma before and after *Patty*. Options A and B are incorrect because a quotation mark and an exclamation point are not needed. The sentence is not correct as it is (option D), because a comma is needed. [Commas]

34. **F** In this direct quotation, a comma should be placed after the phrase *Dave asked*. Options G and H are not correct because a question mark and a quotation mark are not needed. The sentence is not correct as it is (option J), because a comma is needed. [Quotation Marks]

35. **D** Because this sentence is a statement, it should end with a period. Options A, B, and C are unnecessary punctuation marks. [End Marks]

36. **H** This sentence contains a series of four sports. There should be a series comma after *basketball*, the second sport in the series. Options F and G are not correct because neither a question mark nor a quotation mark is needed. The sentence is not correct as it is (option J), because a comma is needed. [Commas]

37. **B** This sentence expresses strong emotion and should end with an exclamation point. Options A and C are not correct because neither a comma nor a quotation mark is needed. The sentence is not correct as it is (option D), because an exclamation point is needed. [End Marks]

38. **J** Option J is the correct topic sentence, because it introduces the subject of beach vacations. Options F, G, and H are about different aspects of vacations, but not about beach vacations in particular. [Topic Sentence]

39. **A** Option A is correct because it explains how Sadie ended up under the tree barking at a cat. Options B and C are not correct because these events would have occurred *before* or *while* Sam let her out the door, not *after*. Option D does not explain how the cat entered the story. [Sequence]

40. **H** The final sentence should explain what Jason did in the barbershop. Options F and G are events that occurred while Jason was in the barbershop. Option J skips over Artie's seeing Jason's green hair. [Sequence]

41. **B** This paragraph describes the steps for making popcorn. Therefore, the topic sentence must introduce the subject of making popcorn. Options A, C, and D focus on popcorn itself, not on how to make it on the stove. [Topic Sentence]

42. **G** The apostrophe in *town's* shows ownership. In option F, *Isnt'* should be *Isn't*. In option H, the apostrophe is left out of the contraction. In option J, the apostrophe that belongs before the *s* in *years* is missing. [Apostrophe]

43. **C** Option C correctly ends with a question mark. Option A should have a period, while option B is a question without a question mark. Option D is a statement and should end with a period. [Question Marks]

44. **J** Option J is the only complete sentence. Option F should be two sentences, broken between *movies* and *we*. Option G is a run-on sentence; the first letter of the second sentence should be *I*. Option H is a fragment and lacks a subject. [Sentence Recognition]

45. **C** Option C includes quotation marks around the coach's exact words, a comma after *game,* and a period after *explained*. Option A has a period, not a comma, after *won*. In option B, the question mark should follow *this,* not *asked*. In option D, the closing quotation marks should follow the comma after *game*. [Quotation Marks]

46. **J** Option J correctly includes the past perfect *had hoped*. Option F should have the past perfect tense *had started*. In option G, the verb should be *had planned*. Option H should use the singular verb *has* to agree with *report*. [Perfect Tense]

47. **D** In option A, *mexican* should be capitalized. In option B, *Daughter* should not be capitalized, and in option C, *alan* should be capitalized. [Capitalization]

48. **H** *Raised* is the correct past tense form of *raise*. In option F, *rised* should be *raised*. The verb in option

G should be *raised,* and the verb in option J should be *rise.* [Easily Confused Verbs]

49. B Option B includes the correct form for city and state; it has a comma after the city name. In option A, there should be a comma after *Atlanta.* In option C, the colon should be a comma. In option D, the semicolon should be a comma. [Commas]

50. H Option H expresses a complete thought with a subject and a verb. Option F has no subject, while options G and J lack a verb. [Sentence Recognition]

51. D Option D correctly ends with an exclamation point. Option A is a question and should end with a question mark. Options B and C have no end marks. They should end with a period. [End Marks]

52. J In option J, the contraction *we'll* has the apostrophe in the correct place. In option F, the correct contraction is *should've.* In option G, the correct contraction is *Aren't,* and in option H, the correct contraction is *It's.* [Apostrophe]

53. A In option A, *Valentine's* and *Day* correctly begin with capital letters. In option B, *street* should be capitalized. *Holiday* should not begin with a capital letter in option C. In option D, *st. patrick's day* should be capitalized. [Capitalization]

54. J In option J, *it* agrees with *car.* In option F, *they* does not agree with *car. Keys* and *it* do not agree in option G. In option H, *Mr. Chang and his sisters* is plural, while *her* is singular. [Antecedent Agreement]

55. C Option C is a complete sentence. Option A lacks a verb, while option B lacks a subject. Option D is a run-on sentence and should be divided with a period between *1918* and *Babe Ruth.* [Sentence Recognition]

Appendix

Comparative and Superlative Adjectives

Base Adjective	Comparative	Superlative
large	larger	largest
young	younger	youngest
beautiful	more beautiful	most beautiful
expensive	less expensive	least expensive

Choosing Between Adjectives and Adverbs

Adjectives	Adverbs
Describe nouns and pronouns	Describe verbs and adjectives
Example: The fast car sped around the dangerous curve.	Example: The car took off suddenly and sped dangerously around the curve.
Often end in –ful, –ous, –ish, –y	Often end in –ly

TABE Review: Usage
(pages 32–33)

1 Ⓐ Ⓑ Ⓒ Ⓓ
2 Ⓕ Ⓖ Ⓗ Ⓙ
3 Ⓐ Ⓑ Ⓒ Ⓓ
4 Ⓕ Ⓖ Ⓗ Ⓙ
5 Ⓐ Ⓑ Ⓒ Ⓓ
6 Ⓕ Ⓖ Ⓗ Ⓙ
7 Ⓐ Ⓑ Ⓒ Ⓓ
8 Ⓕ Ⓖ Ⓗ Ⓙ
9 Ⓐ Ⓑ Ⓒ Ⓓ
10 Ⓕ Ⓖ Ⓗ Ⓙ
11 Ⓐ Ⓑ Ⓒ Ⓓ
12 Ⓕ Ⓖ Ⓗ Ⓙ
13 Ⓐ Ⓑ Ⓒ Ⓓ
14 Ⓕ Ⓖ Ⓗ Ⓙ
Stop

TABE Review: Sentence Formation
(page 46)

1 Ⓐ Ⓑ Ⓒ Ⓓ
2 Ⓕ Ⓖ Ⓗ Ⓙ
3 Ⓐ Ⓑ Ⓒ Ⓓ
4 Ⓕ Ⓖ Ⓗ Ⓙ
5 Ⓐ Ⓑ Ⓒ Ⓓ
6 Ⓕ Ⓖ Ⓗ Ⓙ
Stop

TABE Review: Paragraph Development *(page 55)*

1 Ⓐ Ⓑ Ⓒ Ⓓ
2 Ⓕ Ⓖ Ⓗ Ⓙ
3 Ⓐ Ⓑ Ⓒ Ⓓ
4 Ⓕ Ⓖ Ⓗ Ⓙ
Stop

TABE Review: Capitalization and Punctuation *(page 62)*

1 Ⓐ Ⓑ Ⓒ Ⓓ
2 Ⓕ Ⓖ Ⓗ Ⓙ
3 Ⓐ Ⓑ Ⓒ Ⓓ
4 Ⓕ Ⓖ Ⓗ Ⓙ
5 Ⓐ Ⓑ Ⓒ Ⓓ
6 Ⓕ Ⓖ Ⓗ Ⓙ
Stop

TABE Review: Writing Conventions *(page 69)*

1 Ⓐ Ⓑ Ⓒ Ⓓ
2 Ⓕ Ⓖ Ⓗ Ⓙ
3 Ⓐ Ⓑ Ⓒ Ⓓ
4 Ⓕ Ⓖ Ⓗ Ⓙ
5 Ⓐ Ⓑ Ⓒ Ⓓ
6 Ⓕ Ⓖ Ⓗ Ⓙ
Stop

TABE Review: Spelling
(pages 73–74)

1 Ⓐ Ⓑ Ⓒ Ⓓ
2 Ⓕ Ⓖ Ⓗ Ⓙ
3 Ⓐ Ⓑ Ⓒ Ⓓ
4 Ⓕ Ⓖ Ⓗ Ⓙ
5 Ⓐ Ⓑ Ⓒ Ⓓ
6 Ⓕ Ⓖ Ⓗ Ⓙ
7 Ⓐ Ⓑ Ⓒ Ⓓ
8 Ⓕ Ⓖ Ⓗ Ⓙ
9 Ⓐ Ⓑ Ⓒ Ⓓ
10 Ⓕ Ⓖ Ⓗ Ⓙ
11 Ⓐ Ⓑ Ⓒ Ⓓ
12 Ⓕ Ⓖ Ⓗ Ⓙ
13 Ⓐ Ⓑ Ⓒ Ⓓ
14 Ⓕ Ⓖ Ⓗ Ⓙ
15 Ⓐ Ⓑ Ⓒ Ⓓ
16 Ⓕ Ⓖ Ⓗ Ⓙ
17 Ⓐ Ⓑ Ⓒ Ⓓ
18 Ⓕ Ⓖ Ⓗ Ⓙ
19 Ⓐ Ⓑ Ⓒ Ⓓ
Stop

Performance Assessment: Language
(pages 75–84)

A Ⓐ Ⓑ Ⓒ Ⓓ
B Ⓕ Ⓖ Ⓗ Ⓙ
C Ⓐ Ⓑ Ⓒ Ⓓ
D Ⓕ Ⓖ Ⓗ Ⓙ
1 Ⓐ Ⓑ Ⓒ Ⓓ
2 Ⓕ Ⓖ Ⓗ Ⓙ
3 Ⓐ Ⓑ Ⓒ Ⓓ
4 Ⓕ Ⓖ Ⓗ Ⓙ
5 Ⓐ Ⓑ Ⓒ Ⓓ
6 Ⓕ Ⓖ Ⓗ Ⓙ
7 Ⓐ Ⓑ Ⓒ Ⓓ
Go On

8 Ⓕ Ⓖ Ⓗ Ⓙ
9 Ⓐ Ⓑ Ⓒ Ⓓ
10 Ⓕ Ⓖ Ⓗ Ⓙ
11 Ⓐ Ⓑ Ⓒ Ⓓ
12 Ⓕ Ⓖ Ⓗ Ⓙ
13 Ⓐ Ⓑ Ⓒ Ⓓ
14 Ⓕ Ⓖ Ⓗ Ⓙ
15 Ⓐ Ⓑ Ⓒ Ⓓ
16 Ⓕ Ⓖ Ⓗ Ⓙ
17 Ⓐ Ⓑ Ⓒ Ⓓ
18 Ⓕ Ⓖ Ⓗ Ⓙ
19 Ⓐ Ⓑ Ⓒ Ⓓ
20 Ⓕ Ⓖ Ⓗ Ⓙ
21 Ⓐ Ⓑ Ⓒ Ⓓ
22 Ⓕ Ⓖ Ⓗ Ⓙ
23 Ⓐ Ⓑ Ⓒ Ⓓ
24 Ⓕ Ⓖ Ⓗ Ⓙ
25 Ⓐ Ⓑ Ⓒ Ⓓ
26 Ⓕ Ⓖ Ⓗ Ⓙ
27 Ⓐ Ⓑ Ⓒ Ⓓ
28 Ⓕ Ⓖ Ⓗ Ⓙ
29 Ⓐ Ⓑ Ⓒ Ⓓ
30 Ⓕ Ⓖ Ⓗ Ⓙ
31 Ⓐ Ⓑ Ⓒ Ⓓ
32 Ⓕ Ⓖ Ⓗ Ⓙ
33 Ⓐ Ⓑ Ⓒ Ⓓ
34 Ⓕ Ⓖ Ⓗ Ⓙ
35 Ⓐ Ⓑ Ⓒ Ⓓ
36 Ⓕ Ⓖ Ⓗ Ⓙ
37 Ⓐ Ⓑ Ⓒ Ⓓ
38 Ⓕ Ⓖ Ⓗ Ⓙ
39 Ⓐ Ⓑ Ⓒ Ⓓ
40 Ⓕ Ⓖ Ⓗ Ⓙ
41 Ⓐ Ⓑ Ⓒ Ⓓ
42 Ⓕ Ⓖ Ⓗ Ⓙ
43 Ⓐ Ⓑ Ⓒ Ⓓ
44 Ⓕ Ⓖ Ⓗ Ⓙ
45 Ⓐ Ⓑ Ⓒ Ⓓ
46 Ⓕ Ⓖ Ⓗ Ⓙ
47 Ⓐ Ⓑ Ⓒ Ⓓ
48 Ⓕ Ⓖ Ⓗ Ⓙ
49 Ⓐ Ⓑ Ⓒ Ⓓ
50 Ⓕ Ⓖ Ⓗ Ⓙ
51 Ⓐ Ⓑ Ⓒ Ⓓ
52 Ⓕ Ⓖ Ⓗ Ⓙ
53 Ⓐ Ⓑ Ⓒ Ⓓ
54 Ⓕ Ⓖ Ⓗ Ⓙ
55 Ⓐ Ⓑ Ⓒ Ⓓ
Stop